Modern Middle East Nations

AND THEIR STRATEGIC PLACE IN THE WORLD

SAUDI ARABIA

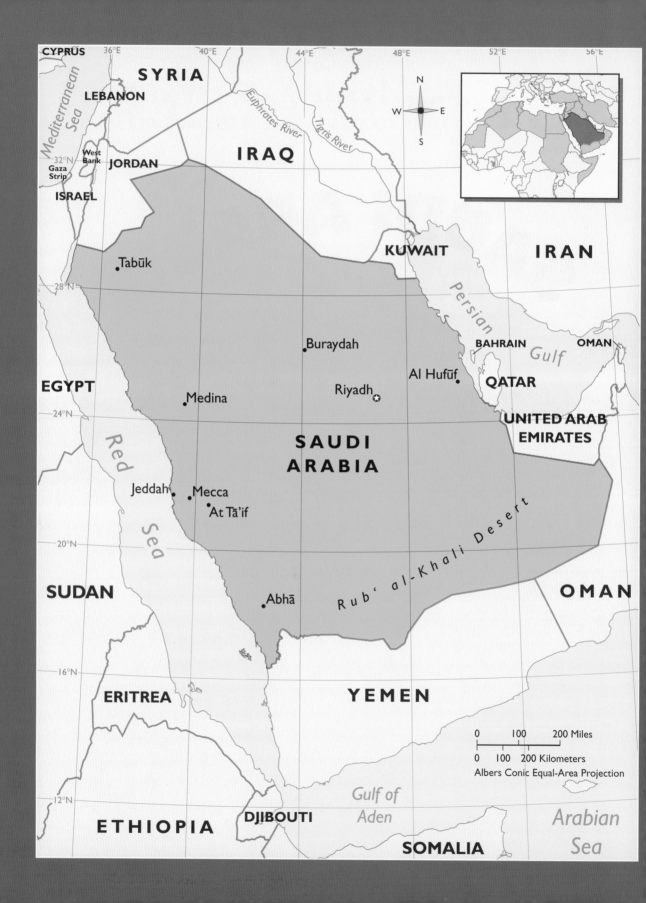

Modern Middle East Nations
AND THEIR STRATEGIC PLACE IN THE WORLD

SAUDI ARABIA

SUSAN KATZ KEATING

MASON CREST PUBLISHERS
PHILADELPHIA

Produced by OTTN Publishing, Stockton, New Jersey

Mason Crest Publishers
370 Reed Road
Broomall, PA 19008
www.masoncrest.com

· 3 5 7 9 8 6 4 2

Library of Congress Cataloging-in-Publication Data

Keating, Susan Katz.
    Saudi Arabia / Susan Katz Keating.
      p. cm. — (Modern Middle East nations and their strategic
place in the world)
Summary: Discusses the geography, history, economy, government,
religion, people, foreign relations, and major cities of Saudi Arabia.
Includes bibliographical references and index.
    ISBN 1-59084-509-9
1. Saudi Arabia—Juvenile literature.   [1. Saudi Arabia.]
. Title. II. Series.
DS204.25.K43 2003 953.8—dc21

                                    2002013005

TABLE OF CONTENTS

Modern Middle East Nations
AND THEIR STRATEGIC PLACE IN THE WORLD

Dr. Harvey Sicherman, president and director of the Foreign Policy Research Institute, is the author of such books as *America the Vulnerable: Our Military Problems and How to Fix Them* (2002) and *Palestinian Autonomy, Self-Government and Peace* (1993).

Introduction

by Dr. Harvey Sicherman

Situated as it is between Africa, Europe, and the Far East, the Middle East has played a unique role in world history. Often described as the birthplace of religions (notably Judaism, Christianity, and Islam) and the cradle of civilizations (Egypt, Mesopotamia, Persia), this region and its peoples have given humanity some of its most precious possessions. At the same time, the Middle East has had more than its share of conflicts. The area is strewn with the ruins of fortifications and the cemeteries of combatants, not to speak of modern arsenals for war.

Today, more than ever, Americans are aware that events in the Middle East can affect our security and prosperity. The United States has a considerable military, political, and economic presence throughout much of the region. Developments there regularly find their way onto the front pages of our newspapers and the screens of our television sets.

Still, it is fair to say that most Middle Eastern countries remain a mystery, their cultures and religions barely known, their peoples and politics confusing and strange. The purpose of this book series is to change that, to educate the reader in the basic facts about the 23 states and many peoples that make up the region. (For our purpose, the Middle East also includes the North African states linked by ethnicity, language, and religion to the Arabs, as well as Somalia and Mauritania, which are African but share the Muslim religion and are members of the Arab League.) A notable feature of the series is the integration of geography, demography, and history; economics and politics; culture and religion. The careful student will learn much that he or she needs to know about ever so important lands.

A few general observations are in order as an introduction to the subject matter.

The first has to do with history and politics. The modern Middle East is full of ancient sites and peoples who trace their lineage and literature to antiquity. Many commentators also attribute the Middle East's political conflicts to grievances and rivalries from the distant past. While history is often invoked, the truth is that the modern Middle East political system dates only from the 1920s and was largely created by the British and the French, the victors of World War I. Such states as Algeria, Iraq, Israel, Jordan, Kuwait, Saudi Arabia, Syria, Turkey, and the United Arab Emirates did not exist before 1914—they became independent between 1920 and 1971. Others, such as Egypt and Iran, were dominated by outside powers until well after World War II. Before 1914, most of the region's states were either controlled by the Turkish-run Ottoman Empire or owed allegiance to the Ottoman sultan. (The sultan was also the caliph or highest religious authority in Islam, in the line of the prophet Muhammad's successors, according to the beliefs of the majority of Muslims known as the Sunni.) It was this imperial Muslim system that was ended by the largely British military victory over the Ottomans in World War I. Few of the leaders who emerged in the wake of this event were happy with the territories they were assigned or the borders, which were often drawn by Europeans. Yet, the system has endured despite many efforts to change it.

The second observation has to do with economics, demography, and natural resources. The Middle Eastern peoples live in a region of often dramatic geographical contrasts: vast parched deserts and high mountains, some with year-round snow; stone-hard volcanic rifts and lush semi-tropical valleys; extremely dry and extremely wet conditions, sometimes separated by only a few miles; large permanent rivers and wadis, riverbeds dry as a bone until winter rains send torrents of flood from the mountains to the sea. In ancient times, a very skilled agriculture made the Middle East the breadbasket of the Roman Empire, and its trade carried luxury fabrics, foods, and spices both East and West.

Most recently, however, the Middle East has become more known for a single commodity—oil, which is unevenly distributed and largely concentrated in the Persian Gulf and Arabian Peninsula (although large pockets are also to be found in Algeria, Libya, and other sites). There are also new, potentially lucrative offshore gas fields in the Eastern Mediterranean.

This uneven distribution of wealth has been compounded by demographics. Birth rates are very high, but the countries with the most oil are often lightly populated. Over the last decade, Middle East populations under the age of 20 have grown enormously. How will these young people be educated? Where will they work? The failure of most governments in the region to give their people skills and jobs (with notable exceptions such as Israel) has also contributed to large out-migrations. Many have gone to Europe; many others work in other Middle Eastern countries, supporting their families from afar.

Another unsettling situation is the heavy pressure both people and industry have put on vital resources. Chronic water shortages plague the region. Air quality, public sanitation, and health services in the big cities are also seriously overburdened. There are solutions to these problems, but they require a cooperative approach that is sorely lacking.

A third important observation is the role of religion in the Middle East. Americans, who take separation of church and state for granted, should know that most countries in the region either proclaim their countries to be Muslim or allow a very large role for that religion in public life. Among those with predominantly Muslim populations, Turkey alone describes itself as secular and prohibits avowedly religious parties in the political system. Lebanon was a Christian-dominated state, and Israel continues to be a Jewish state. While both strongly emphasize secular politics, religion plays an enormous role in culture, daily life, and legislation. It is also important to recall that Islamic law (*Sharia*) permits people to practice Judaism and Christianity in Muslim states but only as *Dhimmi*, protected but very second-class citizens.

Fourth, the American student of the modern Middle East will be impressed by the varieties of one-man, centralized rule, very unlike the workings of Western democracies. There are monarchies, some with traditional methods of consultation for tribal elders and even ordinary citizens, in Saudi Arabia and many Gulf States; kings with limited but still important parliaments (such as in Jordan and

Morocco); and military and civilian dictatorships, some (such as Syria) even operating on the hereditary principle (Hafez al Assad's son Bashar succeeded him). Turkey is a practicing democracy, although a special role is given to the military that limits what any government can do. Israel operates the freest democracy, albeit constricted by emergency regulations (such as military censorship) due to the Arab-Israeli conflict.

In conclusion, the MODERN MIDDLE EAST NATIONS series will engage imagination and interest simply because it covers an area of such great importance to the United States. Americans may be relative latecomers to the affairs of this region, but our involvement there will endure. We at the Foreign Policy Research Institute hope that these books will kindle a lifelong interest in the fascinating and significant Middle East.

The Shaybah oilfield is one of many in Saudi Arabia. Beneath the sands of this desert country lies about one-quarter of the world's oil reserves. This energy resource has made Saudi Arabia one of the wealthiest nations in the world.

Place in the World

September 2002 marked Saudi Arabia's 70th anniversary as a kingdom, but people have been living in the lands of the present Saudi kingdom for thousands of years. The nation we know today as Saudi Arabia was once a wide-ranging region of small territories ruled by different families.

Those families lived in small settlements mostly near the coast, or traveled from place to place in the desert atop camels. At different times the tribes went to war against or formed alliances with their neighbors. But the ever-shifting relations between these families remained within the boundaries of the Arabian Peninsula, a distinct landform that sits between Africa and the Arab nations of Southwest Asia.

Even as recently as the colonial period, those unfamiliar with the Arabian Peninsula—which before 1932 was known as Arabia—viewed it as an exotic land, filled with mystery. For foreigners, the deserts of Arabia, so remote and forbidding, seemed to shut off access not only to the land, but also to the very people who lived there.

One of the first modern glimpses into this mysterious place was, interestingly, supplied by a one-time British spy and advisor to Arabian rulers. Harry St. John Philby, who fell in love with the land and the people on whom he was supposed to inform, wrote a number of books about the region between 1928 and 1957. These books provided some much needed insight into the land of date palms, camels, and sand dunes.

Today, however, Saudi Arabia is less a mystery. It is very much in the international spotlight, holding a prominent place in world affairs. When journalists, historians, and teachers discuss recent history or current events of the Middle East, the talk frequently touches on Saudi Arabia. The desert country is strategically important, as its rich reserves of oil help many nations—including the United States—meet their energy needs. Saudi Arabia has made efforts to bring peace to the long-standing conflict between Israel and the Palestinians, with varying success. It also has served as a base for American soldiers who protect the region from the threat of aggression from neighboring Iraq.

How did this transformation take place? How did a remote desert land come to occupy such a visible place in international affairs? With no single overriding factor governing these changes, there isn't a simple answer, though Saudi Arabia's oil resources and its key role in the development of Islam are undoubtedly two of the more important factors of change.

THE DISCOVERY OF OIL

Shortly after much of the Arabian Peninsula was united into a single kingdom in 1932, large quantities of oil were discovered in Saudi Arabia. At first, the American explorers who found the oil did not know how much was actually there. As it turned out, the underground mineral lakes were a genuine treasure trove of oil. The Kingdom of Saudi Arabia sits atop more than one-fourth of the world's natural oil reserves. The nation produces millions of barrels of oil per day, and sells its oil and gas in huge quantities to consumers throughout the world. It is the world's largest single exporter of oil and gas. This places Saudi Arabia in a unique position, as it holds control over a much-needed international commodity.

To many people, Saudi Arabia is less important for its oil than for its place as the spiritual center of the Islamic religion. Five times each day, devout Muslims throughout the world face toward Mecca, a city in Saudi Arabia, to pray. Millions of Muslims make pilgrimages to Saudi Arabia each year. The Holy Mosque of Mecca (Masjid al-Haram), pictured here, can accommodate about 700,000 worshipers. It contains the Ka'aba, the most sacred Islamic relic.

The sale of so much oil of course brings in enormous sums of money—so much, in fact, that the once impoverished kingdom has become fabulously wealthy.

That wealth arrived almost overnight. Saudi Arabia's first king, Abd al-Aziz **ibn** Saud, used his newfound riches to build a more modern nation, literally from the ground up. The redevelopment of Saudi Arabia in the middle decades of the 20th century—involving the replacement of desert tents with modern skyscrapers, airports, universities, and other buildings and facilities—is in some estimations one of the greatest physical improvements achieved by any nation in such a short time.

The transformation created an interesting effect. With its newly created high standard of living, the desert kingdom was able to provide for and educate a good number of its citizens. Education brought knowledge, and with it, skills and power. Over time, modernization helped to place Saudi Arabia in a position of influence among neighboring Arab states.

ISLAM'S DEFENDER

But Saudi Arabia's unique place in word affairs is also tied to another factor: its role in the preservation of Islam, one of the world's major religions. Saudi Arabia is the spiritual home of Islam; the religion was actually founded in a town that is now part of Saudi Arabia. As such, Saudi Arabia has an influence on the more than 1 billion people around the globe who practice Islam.

That influence is felt in several ways. First, because the religion was founded on present-day Saudi territory, Saudi Arabia has custody of the two holiest sites of Islam—the cities of Mecca and Medina.

Second, the rulers of Saudi Arabia are deeply concerned about matters—both spiritual and non-spiritual—pertaining to other Muslims (those who follow the teachings of Islam). In the spiritual sense, Saudi Arabia advocates a particular form of Islam. In the non-spiritual, or temporal, sense, the kingdom tries to advance the interests of the Saudi state and Al Saud family. In regard to issues surrounding the oil trade, for example, Saudi Arabia has on occasion taken aggressive actions that have had an impact on world affairs.

But Saudi Arabia is more than just a source of economic or political influence. It is a complex, multifaceted society. It has a fascinating history. It has produced interesting customs and a unique culture. Everything about this desert kingdom—from its culture and religion to its economy and foreign relations—is unique.

A Saudi man visits the local camel market near Riyadh, the capital of Saudi Arabia. With its oil revenues, Saudi Arabia has built modern cities in the desert.

The Land

In 1975, American and Soviet astronauts orbiting the Earth took pictures of the Middle East from their perch in outer space. Later, scientists who looked at the pictures were intrigued to see a network of cracks and fault lines spreading across the region in the shape of a giant fan. The fan shape started in the Golan Heights of Israel and spread north and east across the Arabian Peninsula.

Geologists, who study rocks and rock formations, already knew that the Arabian Peninsula had once been part of Africa. Now, in the pictures from space, the scientists saw the physical signs of the earth's continents in motion. They saw where the massive peninsula, shaped like the side view of a giant snow boot, had rotated away from Africa.

On the western edge, or back heel, of the boot, the rotation had caused an enormous split, known as the Great Rift. Many eons ago, that rift filled with water and became the famed Red Sea. The eastern edge of the peninsula—or, the front slope of the boot—had moved closer to Iran. The boot's "toe" trapped a vast section of ocean into a formation known as the Persian Gulf, also called the Arabian Gulf.

Here on Earth, we don't have an overhead view of the entire Arabian Peninsula. Even without the pictures from outer space, though, we can see how Saudi Arabia—which takes up almost 80 percent of the peninsula—bears the effects of ancient geologic change.

Imagine again the peninsula shaped like a boot. Lay the boot on its side, and lift the heel so that the entire side of the boot slopes downward toward the toe. That is basically how the Arabian Peninsula sits atop the earth, tilted by seismic movements deep below the crust. On the west are high rugged mountains that drop off sharply to the waters of the Red Sea. The entire landmass, which is mostly ancient rock covered by newer rock or sand, tips steadily

This satellite view of the Arabian Peninsula shows a sandstorm blowing across the Persian Gulf.

Most of Saudi Arabia is low-lying sandy desert; the Hejaz mountain range, which contains the country's highest point, runs along the Red Sea on the peninsula's west coast. Most of the country's major oil fields are located near the Persian Gulf; the Shaybah oilfield in the Rub al-Khali desert to the south is one of the more recent fields to be developed.

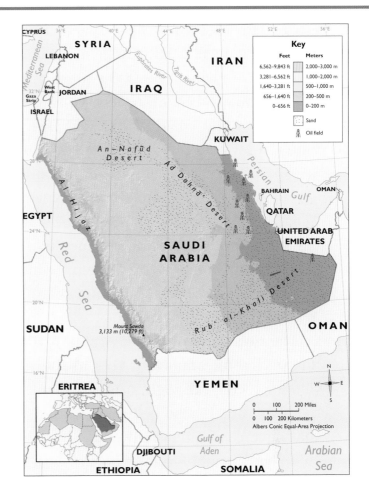

downwards, declining into low beaches on the eastern coast. There, the land is jagged even under the water. The Persian Gulf is filled with beautiful but treacherous coral reefs that can rip right through the hull of a ship.

DESERTS AND MOUNTAINS

Saudi Arabia is one of the driest places in the world. On average, less than five inches of rainfall water the desert kingdom each year. No wonder, then, that much of the country is made up of seemingly endless stretches of sand dunes, salt flats, and gravel plains. One large portion of Saudi Arabia, Rub al-Khali (the Empty Quarter), is so dry and formidable that no one dares venture there alone. The vast sand field covers roughly 212,300 square miles (550,000 square kilometers), a significant chunk of the country, which covers some 869,000 square miles (2,250,000 sq km).

The western region, called the Hejaz, includes a chain of mountains along the coast of the Red Sea. These mountains range in height from between 1,968 feet (600 meters) around Mecca to just over 6,890 feet (2,100 meters) toward the northern areas.

The southern region, which connects with the **Hejaz**, is called Asir. This, too, is a coastal region, with dramatic mountain peaks reaching to 9,842 feet (3,000 meters). The Asir region borders the neighboring country of Yemen, which lies to the southwest. Because Asir receives so much rainfall, it is the only area of Saudi Arabia that has a forest.

The heartland of Saudi Arabia is known as the Najd. This area has played an important role in the nation's politics and history. Geographically, though, it is one giant eroded plateau. It has a few marshes, but is also believed to show the remains of ancient seas that have been long dried up.

To the north, along the border with Iraq and Jordan, is the vast, dune-covered An Nafud Desert, also known as the Great Nafud. (In Arabic, *An Nafud* actually means "desert.") Another large desert is the Ad Dahna, a long, finger-like strip known as the River of Sand. The Ad Dahna runs parallel to the eastern coast, and connects An Nafud with the Empty Quarter.

The sands of An Nafud and Ad Dahna are filled with iron oxide. When the sun is low in the sky, the sun's rays bounce off the iron oxide and cause the metal fragments to glint so that the sand shimmers with red.

A CHALLENGING CLIMATE

Unlike the western United States, whose deserts are interspersed with fresh water sources, Saudi Arabia has no permanent rivers or lakes. Water is scarce and precious. Most of the country's rain falls on the western mountain ranges and trickles underground along the tilted peninsula toward the eastern coast.

Rain prompts the desert to spring briefly to life. Wild plants include desert chamomile, scarlet pimpernel, heliotrope, and wild iris. Desert animals include lizards, porcupines, hedgehogs, and even rabbits.

Sometimes water flows above ground in narrow rivulets, along the remains of ancient riverbeds known as **wadis**. In other places, the water bubbles up to the surface and creates a patch of fertile ground known as an oasis.

The Geography of Saudi Arabia

Location: Middle East, bordering the Persian Gulf and the Red Sea, north of Yemen

Area: slightly more than one-fifth the size of the U.S.
   total: 756,981 square miles (1,960,582 sq km)
   land: 756,981 square miles (1,960,582 sq km)
   water: 0 miles

Borders: Iraq 506 miles (814 km), Jordan 462 miles (744 km), Kuwait 138 miles (222 km), Oman 420 miles (676 km), Qatar 37 miles (60 km), UAE 284 miles (457 km), Yemen 906 miles (1,458 km), coastline 1,640 miles (2,640 km)

Climate: harsh, dry desert with great temperature extremes

Terrain: mostly uninhabited, sandy desert

Elevation extremes:
   lowest point: Persian Gulf—0 feet below sea level
   highest point: Jabal Sawda—10,279 feet (3,133 meters)

Natural hazards: frequent sand and dust storms

Source: Adapted from CIA World Factbook, 2002.

A recreational park in Dammam, on the Persian Gulf. Saudi Arabia has used some of its oil revenues to develop the desert country.

For centuries, wandering **bedouins** used the oases to sustain their families and livestock. Because the land is so harsh, the bedouins relied heavily on the labor of the hardy desert camel, which is famous for being able to live for long periods without drinking water.

The bedouins grew crops where they could. The most plentiful crop was the date palm. The bedouins often survived on a diet of dates and camel milk. Their mode of living was largely determined by changes in weather. If an oasis dried up, they moved to another one.

The country's temperature extremes make living in the more

remote parts even more difficult. Winter in the mountains can be surprisingly cold, with the thermometer dipping below freezing. In the summer the deserts are scorching hot, with temperatures reaching up to 129° Fahrenheit (53° Celsius). Even on the coast, the thermometer can reach up to 120°F (49°C). In the day, the densely humid air is filled with hot mist. At night, the land is blanketed with warm fog.

Weather along the gulf coast is cooled slightly by a northern wind. A coastal wind from the south, though, brings a type of hot weather storm known as a *kauf.* During spring and summer, a strong wind called a *shamal* blows in a northwesterly direction. The *shamal* lasts nearly three months and creates violent, blinding sandstorms.

The feature of the peninsula that has enabled Saudis to overcome the harsh weather conditions is, of course, oil. Most of the oil in Saudi Arabia is in the eastern Al Hasa province. The sale of oil has produced more than enough money to enable the Saudis to irrigate large farms and build comfortable towns and cities. The once-dry land is becoming more fertile. The Saudis are looking for ways to tap into vast reservoirs of water trapped beneath the surface of rock. In the future, the geography of Saudi Arabia may be completely different.

Scientists have predicted at least one long-term geographical change. Geologists who examined the astronauts' space photographs estimated that the Arabian Peninsula will continue to rotate. In another 10 million years, the toe of the "boot" will kick upwards, closing off the Persian Gulf and turning it into a lake.

It is fascinating to think of what might happen in the future. It is equally intriguing to look into the past, particularly into the history of the Desert Kingdom, Saudi Arabia.

U.S. Marines disembark from an amphibious transport at Dhahran, Saudi Arabia, in September 1990. These marines were among the thousands of American soldiers sent to protect Saudi Arabia after Iraq's August 1990 invasion of Kuwait; their deployment was called Operation Desert Shield.

History

At first glance, it seems as if Saudi Arabia is very young for a country. The modern nation was only founded in 1932. Some people alive today are older than the Kingdom of Saudi Arabia.

The political state itself is young, but Saudi Arabia's traditions and culture are old. The founding of the modern state can be traced to events that took place more than 1,000 years ago. The nation's cultural roots stretch back even further. It is interesting to see that by looking into events from Saudi Arabia's past, we can gain a better understanding of events that take place today.

In ancient times, tribes of **nomads** roamed those parts of the Arabian Peninsula that could sustain life. People also settled in villages or towns along the coast. The settled Arabs and foreigners exchanged a wide variety of products, including textiles, spices, and agricultural goods. The trading partners came to Arabia via various ports along the Red Sea or the Persian Gulf, arriving from places such as Byzantium, China, Egypt, Greece, and Rome. Few of the Arab merchants ventured inland, though; the territory was simply too harsh and forbidding. The hardy camel was of little help: the animal could not carry enough goods to justify a long and dangerous journey across the barren desert.

THE CAMEL AND THE ANCIENT TRADE

Around 1000 B.C., Arabs developed a type of saddle that enabled camels to carry large cargoes. The new saddle created new trading possibilities. Merchants could now load their camels with huge piles of goods for sale. Aided by their four-footed "ships of the desert," they immediately set out to forge new trade routes.

The camel caravans stopped to rest at various sites along the way. One of those sites was at an oasis called Yathrib, situated about midway up the peninsula and roughly 150 miles (241 km) inland. Another site was known as Mecca (sometimes spelled *Makkah*). Every year, Arabs made a pilgrimage, or journey, to Mecca, where they worshipped their gods at an ancient shrine known as the Ka'aba.

Mecca became a lively center of commerce. Tribes settled there and began to send out their own caravans to trade with cities in neighboring Yemen and Syria. One tribe in particular, the Quraysh, became quite powerful.

THE BIRTH OF ISLAM

In 570, a Quraysh woman gave birth to a son named **Muhammad**. The baby would grow to become the single most powerful influence on the history of Saudi Arabia.

According to Islamic tradition, when Muhammad was 40 years old the angel Gabriel appeared to him in the wilderness and told him to spread the word that there was only one God (called Allah).

Muhammad followed Gabriel's instructions, and as he continued to deliver the angel's messages, the people of Mecca grew divided. Some believed Muhammad spoke an important truth. Others thought he was a troublemaker.

Muhammad's enemies decided to kill him. Muhammad learned of the plot, so he and his followers fled Mecca for the town of Yathrib (known today as Medina). This flight became known as the *Hijrah*, or migration. To this day, the year of the *Hijrah*—A.D. 622 according to the Western calendar—marks the first year of the Islamic calendar.

This page from a 12th-century Arabic manuscript shows a caravan passing a fortified town. With the domestication of the camel some 3,000 years ago, trading became an important part of life in the desert, and helped spread ideas, cultural beliefs, and technology throughout the Arabian Peninsula.

The Prophet's Mosque (Masjid Nabvi) in Medina is a huge structure that holds up to 1 million worshippers. It is considered one of the most sacred sites in Islam. Muhammad lived in Medina from A.D. 622 to 629; it was during his time in this city that his followers grew strong enough to conquer Mecca and eventually spread their religion throughout the Arabian Peninsula and beyond.

Muhammad and his followers went to war against their opponents in Mecca. After many battles, Muhammad emerged victorious. He returned to rule Mecca, while his army continued to conquer other towns. Christians and Jews were allowed to retain their own religions, but pagans were forced to practice Muhammad's new faith, Islam, the followers of which were now commonly known as Muslims.

Muhammad died in 632, but Islam still continued to spread at a rapid rate. Less than 100 years after the founding of Islam, Muslims controlled an empire that reached from Spain and across Arabia to Pakistan and even parts of China. Mecca and Medina became holy cities. In Mecca, an old tradition was transformed. Whereas Arab pagans once made pilgrimages to worship at the Ka'aba, Muslims now traveled in great numbers to worship at Mecca, which became known as a holy city.

All Muslims agreed that their prophet was Muhammad, but they disagreed on how to interpret his teachings. The Islamic world soon split into religious factions after his death. Most Muslims followed a branch of the faith known as **Sunni** Islam; a smaller group broke away to establish their own form of the religion, known as **Shia** Islam. Over the centuries, other forms of Islam, such as Ibadi, developed as well.

WAHHABISM AND THE AL-SAUD

In the early 18th century, a religious thinker named Muhammad ibn Abd al-Wahhab preached that Muslims had fallen away from the true faith. Wahhab preached for a return to the fundamentals of Islam. He was particularly harsh in his criticisms of Shiites—Muslims who follow Shia Islam—who paid homage to shrines and saints. Wahhab preached against Shia Islam and even began to destroy some Shia shrines.

The Shiites drove Wahhab from where he was preaching. Wahhab went to Diriyah, a town in the Najd that is near the present-day capital of Riyadh. There, Wahhab joined forces with a tribal leader named Muhammad ibn Saud. The two men agreed on many things, including their distaste for Shia and their ideas on how to practice Islam. Together, they formed a pact: they would build a kingdom ruled by strict Islamic law.

Muhammad ibn Saud died in 1765, but his descendants continued his quest. Empowered by its version of Islam, known as **Wahhabism**, the **Al Saud** family took control of much of the Najd. The family made their headquarters at Diriyah. From there, they ventured out to enforce Wahhabism, destroying Shia shrines in their path. The Al Saud then turned their sights on the western region, the Hejaz.

Saudi Arabia, founded and run by the House of Saud, is the only country in the world that is named after its ruling family.

THE OTTOMAN EMPIRE AND THE AL-RASHID

At the time, the Turkish-based **Ottoman Empire** had great influence over large portions of the Middle East and Arabia. The Ottomans felt threatened by the Al Saud family's ever-growing power. They knew that their own resources were already stretched too thinly, however, and so did not want to take on the Al Saud directly. Instead, they directed one of their Egyptian underlings, who commanded the Ottoman stronghold in Egypt, to recapture the Hejaz.

During the first decades of the 19th century, the Ottoman-ruled Egyptian forces battled the Al Saud. In that time, both Wahhab and a succession of Al Saud leaders died. The enemy compiled victory after victory. The Al Saud fled to their old home base in Diriyah. In 1818, the Ottoman-backed Egyptians captured Diriyah. They completely destroyed the city, tearing down buildings and even killing the lush palm groves.

Ancient forts near Diriyah, the first capital of the Al Saud. The city is located in a wadi, or dry riverbed, near the present-day capital Riyadh. Diriyah was settled in the early 15th century by the ancestors of Saudi Arabia's first king, Abd al-Aziz. The buildings in Dariyah are made of mud, straw, and seashells.

The Al Saud and the Ottomans continued to grapple for control of the region. At various times, the Al Saud and the Ottomans came to somewhat peaceable terms with one another; at other times, they fought bitterly. The Al Saud also fought among themselves. The Ottomans took advantage of that internal rivalry, and played the quarrelling factions against one another.

The Al Saud did some manipulating of their own. Further to the east, Great Britain was heavily involved in India. The British feared that the Ottomans might expand their influence toward India, and interfere with Britain's development of the Suez Canal, an important waterway project that would shorten the trade route from Britain to India by 6,000 miles (9,656 km). From the 1830s through the 1880s, the Al Saud used this tension to their own advantage. The Arabs helped the British thwart the Ottomans, while they gained their own ground against them on other fronts.

An iron Turkish helmet ornamented with silver, circa 1500. Based in Turkey, the Ottoman Empire ruled much of eastern Europe, north Africa, and the Arabian Peninsula from the 15th century until the early 20th century.

Meanwhile, a rival Arab family, the **Al Rashid**, gradually established themselves in the Najd. They took over the city of Riyadh. Around 1891, the defeated Al Saud fled into exile in neighboring Kuwait.

In 1902, a young man named Abd al-Aziz ibn Saud vowed to reconquer the territory once ruled by his family. Operating from exile in Kuwait, Abd al-Aziz raised a small army with which he captured Riyadh. He continued his family's earlier relationship with the British. Later, he drove the Ottomans out of the east coast town of Al Hufuf. From his new base in Riyadh, Abd al-Aziz gradually took over much of the Najd.

While Abd al-Aziz was gaining power in Arabia, the situation in Europe grew increasingly unstable. The powerful nations of the West were at odds with one another. By the 19th century, the Ottoman Empire was known as the "sick man" of Europe. It was losing its power and land, and many competing European countries were eager to pick up the empire's former territories. Eventually, the turmoil in Europe erupted into World War I.

ABD AL-AZIZ AND THE NEW KINGDOM

When the war ended, parts of Arabia and the Middle East were redivided. The new League of Nations system produced two land mandates: France had one for Lebanon and Syria, and Great Britain had one for Iraq and Palestine, which it divided into Palestine and Transjordan. The European countries virtually owned the countries, while permitting their leaders a moderate level of governance.

Great Britain was less involved in the affairs of the Arabian Peninsula. Abd al-Aziz took advantage of Great Britain's neutrality, as well as the Ottoman Empire's own preoccupation with Europe before and during World War I, to further establish his kingdom. Between 1902 and 1926, he took control over territory stretching all the way to the Red Sea, on the western coast of the peninsula. Among his new conquests were the holy cities of Mecca and Medina, which were captured in 1924.

Like many of the Al Saud before him, Abd al-Aziz followed very closely the teachings of Wahhabism. He remembered his ancestor's original pact: to found a nation based on Islam. As such, he considered himself not just the leader of a country, but also a religious guardian, the "custodian of the two holy mosques."

In his rise to power, Abd al-Aziz had many allies, but he also faced fierce resistance against Jordan, Iraq, and Yemen that in some ways foreshadows present-day events in the Middle East.

Within the Najd and Hejaz, a religious faction known as the **Ikhwan**, who had previously supported Abd al-Aziz, now turned hostile. The Ikhwan believed that the Saudi leader did not properly follow the teachings of Islam, nor did they feel that Abd al-Aziz was strict enough. In much the same way that some groups in the modern Middle East object to any dealings with the West, the Ikhwan protested against Abd al-Aziz's friendly relations with Great Britain.

In addition, the Ikhwan were angry that Abd al-Aziz had brought modern inventions—such as the telegraph, the telephone, and the automobile—to Saudi Arabia. Furthermore, they thought Abd al-Aziz was weak for permitting people to follow different forms of Islam, such as Shia. The Ikhwan insisted that Abd al-Aziz convert the Shiites to Wahhabi Islam, and kill those who refused to be converted. Abd al-Aziz and the Ikhwan went to war. Influential religious scholars, known as the **ulema**, intervened to help settle the dispute. By 1930, Abd al-Aziz had

During the 1920s Abd al-Aziz ibn Saud (1880–1953) reconquered much of the Arabian territory his family had once controlled. He established the kingdom of Saudi Arabia in 1932. His descendants, the Al Saud family, continue to rule the country today.

put down the Ikhwan revolt.

In 1932, Abd al-Aziz proclaimed the formation of the Kingdom of Saudi Arabia, with himself as the new monarch. True to the pact between Muhammad ibn Abd al-Wahhab and Muhammad ibn Saud, the new kingdom was based on the teachings of Wahhabi Islam. Abd al-Aziz did not write a special constitution with which to govern his nation. Instead, he decided to use the Islamic holy book, the Qur'an (or Koran), as the Saudi Arabian constitution.

Abd al-Aziz soon went to war against Yemen. In another move that foreshadowed current practices, Saudi Arabia obtained a large loan and bought foreign military equipment to use against the enemy. The war soon ended, but to this day, the border between Saudi Arabia and Yemen is regularly contested.

Even with his fledgling nation at peace, though, the new king faced difficult challenges. In the 1930s, the world plunged into economic depression. A large percentage of Muslims could not afford to make the pilgrimage to Mecca, so many Arabs of Saudi Arabia no longer earned money from services provided to those pilgrims. Many of those Arabs could not even afford to feed their families, and so they went to their king for help. Abd al-Aziz provided them with food—sometimes, he fed as many as 2,000 people per day.

Even while the Arab people struggled to survive the depression, though, events were taking place that would soon catapult the country to unheard-of levels of wealth. A few years earlier, just before World War I, geologists had discovered oil reserves on the Iranian side of the Persian Gulf. They suspected that they would also find oil beneath the ground in Saudi Arabia. In the early 1930s, those suspicions were confirmed. Prospectors for the Standard Oil Company of California discovered a number of oil pockets in Saudi Arabia.

As in the past, the hardy camel was pressed into service. Long caravans of lumbering beasts carted geological equipment into the desert. There, the company found vast underground lakes filled with valuable oil. Before long, oil wells sprang up across the desert, and as oil flowed out of the country, huge quantities of money flowed into the nation's treasury.

Abd al-Aziz began to build roads and systems of communication. He spent money on health care, agriculture, and education. In a few short years, Saudi Arabia made great strides toward modernization.

This 1923 photograph of Arab leaders includes (seated, left to right) King Faisal I of Iraq, Emir Abdullah I of Transjordan, and King Ali of the Hejaz (a short-lived Arab kingdom that is now part of Saudi Arabia). All were sons of Hussein bin Ali, the sharif of Mecca, an Arab leader who assisted Great Britain during the First World War by staging the Arab Revolt against the Ottoman Turks in 1916. After the war, the grateful allies granted regional power to Hussein's clan, the Al Hashem. However, Hashemite rule did not last long in Saudi Arabia.

After World War II, another event took place that would have an overpowering influence on the current world situation. In the aftermath of Hitler's atrocities against millions of Jews, the Western powers agreed to help form a Jewish state. The state would be located in the ancient Jewish homeland in Palestine. On Valentine's Day in 1945, President Franklin D. Roosevelt himself met with Abd al-Aziz on board a ship in the Suez Canal. The American president asked Abd al-Aziz to support the formation of a new Jewish state, Israel. Abd al-Aziz refused, saying that Arabs were not responsible for crimes committed by Germany. Israel was established anyway, and its presence would become a subject of great conflict that persists to the present day.

Abd al-Aziz followed the custom of polygamy, whereby a man is allowed more than one wife at a time. According to one biographer, Abd al-Aziz and his dozens of wives produced 34 sons and an untold number of daughters. When he died in 1953, his oldest surviving son, Saud bin Abd al-Aziz, became king.

KING SAUD

The new king, known as Saud, used the country's treasury as if it were his personal bank account. He bought clothing, jewels, and fancy cars, spending huge sums of money on himself and his wives and children. He built 25 palaces and filled them with luxurious goods. As was the custom in Saudi Arabia at the time, King Saud had black slaves. Others in the enormous Saud family looked on in horror as the king depleted the nation's bank accounts.

When neighboring Syria and Egypt merged to form the United Arab Republic in 1958, King Saud was accused of trying to stop the merger by plotting the murder of Egyptian leader Gamal Abdel Nasser. Nothing developed from the accusation, but tension still remained high between the countries.

The Middle East became increasingly volatile. In 1962, civil war broke out in Yemen. Egypt and Saudi Arabia lined up on opposing sides of the Yemeni conflict. Saudi Arabia needed a strong leader to help mediate in Yemen and in other potentially dangerous places. Yet Saud did little besides continuing his spending spree. In 1964, the extended Saud family, fed up with Saud's recklessness, enlisted the help of Muslim religious leaders and forced the king off the throne. The coup was successful and Saud's brother Faisal became king.

KING FAISAL

Many changes took place under Faisal's reign. He allowed the first television broadcasts, permitted girls to attend school, and abolished slavery. Some of those changes brought controversy. In 1965, a group of Saudi fundamentalists were so enraged by the television broadcasts that they attacked the television station. Some of the attackers were killed in a shoot-out with police—an act that would have tragic repercussions for Faisal 10 years later.

Meanwhile, Faisal emerged as a leader not just in Saudi Arabia, but also in the Arab world at large. He assisted in writing a peace plan with Yemen, and helped form the Organization of the Islamic Conference, which promotes cooperation among Muslim countries.

In June 1967, four Arab nations—Egypt, Jordan, Syria, and Iraq—went to war against Israel. Known alternately as the Six-Day War and the June 1967 War, it officially began on June 5 and ended on June 10. The United States supported Israel in the conflict, though its military did not become involved. A number of Arab countries retaliated by withholding petroleum sales to the West. Faisal later persuaded his fellow Arab leaders to resume the petroleum shipments.

In 1973, though, Faisal decided to once again use oil as an economic weapon. Incited by the United States' continued support of Israel, Saudi Arabia and other Arab nations cut back on oil ship-ments to the West. Some oil was sold to the West, but at greatly

increased prices. The price of a barrel of oil was $3 in 1972; it rose
to $12 by 1974. Subsequently, gasoline prices rose from less than
30¢ a gallon to more than $1 a gallon, though the increase was in
part due to mismanagement by federal agencies.

The oil embargo caused an enormous crisis. Governments
imposed strict rules on energy conservation. In Great Britain, police
officers knocked on peoples' doors at night and told them to unplug
their Christmas lights. Throughout the United States, gas stations,
citing pressure to retain their fuel supply, raised their prices to previously unheard-of rates. Many adult Americans today remember
the long lines for gasoline at service stations, the high prices, and
the shock of sometimes not even being able to buy gas at all.

In 1975, Faisal's progress as a committed leader was tragically
cut short. A nephew of King Faisal's, disgruntled over the execution
of his brother for his part in the 1965 television station attack,
decided to take revenge. He murdered the Saudi monarch. Faisal's
brother Khalid was then crowned king.

KING KHALID

Khalid ascended the throne during the Cold War between the
United States and its rival superpower, the Soviet Union. The two
world powers did not actually go to war but remained enemies.
Khalid knew that the Middle East, with its vast oil reserves, would be
a great prize for the Soviets. In order to help keep the Soviets at bay,
Khalid forged closer ties with the United States. Eventually, the
Americans sold high-powered F-15 jet fighter aircraft, plus sophisti-
cated attack-detection aircraft, to Saudi Arabia.

The short peaceful period following Khalid's ascension was dis-
rupted by internal religious dissent. In November 1979, hundreds
of armed dissidents seized Saudi Arabia's most holy site, the Grand
Mosque in Mecca. Many of the dissidents belonged to old Ikhwan
families. The rebels denounced the ruling House of Saud, accusing

it of not properly enforcing the teachings of Islam.

The rebels held the mosque for 10 days. The siege presented a huge problem for the Saudi government. The rebels were so fierce that Khalid knew he could not capture them without bloodshed. But the Saudi constitution, in accordance with the Qur'an, forbade anyone from shedding blood at holy sites. Because the Grand Mosque was the holiest of Muslim sites, it was a grievous crime to stage an attack at the mosque, even if the purpose of the attack was to evict angry rebels.

Khalid appealed to the *ulema* for help. After much consideration, the *ulema* issued a ruling permitting the military to enter the mosque with weapons. French commando troops were called in to help liberate the mosque. Khalid's troops killed 117 rebels, and captured 63. Those 63 were taken to four different cities, where their heads were chopped off in public.

A long line of cars forms at a gas station as drivers wait to purchase gas during the 1973–74 oil crisis. The Arab oil embargo led to shortages and increased prices, and helped push the U.S. economy into a recession.

Saudi Arabia faced other difficult problems during this time. In the eastern province of Al Qatif, Shiite Muslims complained bitterly about being mistreated by the government. Influenced by the Shiite victories in nearby Iran, where the fundamentalist sect had taken over the country in 1979, Shiites in Saudi Arabia began staging aggressive protests.

Khalid sent some 20,000 troops to battle the Shiites. In the end, though, the king could not chop the heads off all the members of an entire religious group. When the riots ended, Khalid acknowledged that the Shiites did indeed have valid complaints. He responded by doing much to improve conditions in Shiite towns. Reforms included the building of schools and hospitals and the installation of modern electricity and water supplies.

Over the course of the next few years, turmoil was constant throughout the Middle East. Iraq attacked Iran in 1980, leading to an eight-year war between the two countries. In Lebanon, a cease-fire to halt a long-standing civil war was broken and fighting resumed during the 1980s. Palestinians and Jews remained at odds over Israel. Libya continually stirred up opposition against Israel. Shiite dissidents tried to take over the island nation of Bahrain. Syria signed a friendship pact with the Soviet Union, which upset the Soviet Union's adversaries in the Middle East. And, in a move that made the region even more volatile, the Soviet Union invaded Afghanistan in 1979.

The entire region, it seemed, was consumed with deadly hostility. The Middle East was like a bomb ready to explode.

Khalid and his brother, Fahd, became increasingly involved in international affairs. They hosted international conferences of Muslim leaders, and advocated for cooperation among Muslim states. The two brothers were involved in the 1981 formation of the Gulf Cooperation Council, an organization designed to help foster friendship among six nations of the Arabian Peninsula. Those nations were Bahrain, Kuwait, Oman, Qatar, Saudi Arabia, and the United Arab Emirates. Among their chief concerns were economic and defense policies—and the handling of Iran.

KING FAHD

When Khalid died in 1982, Fahd became king. Over the next decade, Fahd faced more internal and international crises. Internally, the issue of women's rights came to a head. Saudi Arabia remains the only Muslim country with a law prohibiting women to drive, and that law is strictly enforced. In 1990, a group of women marched into the streets of the capital city, Riyadh, and demanded that they be granted the right to drive cars.

Whereas people in the West might think it preposterous that women should not be allowed to drive, Saudi officials were appalled at what they considered to be an audacious request. The women in the protest were fired from their jobs. Their passports were taken away. Five months later, Fahd softened his stance—somewhat. He restored the women's jobs with back pay and returned their passports. But he held firm on withholding their right to drive.

Bigger problems loomed over Saudi Arabia. In 1990, Iraqi leader Saddam Hussein invaded Kuwait. He declared that he had annexed the tiny country as a province of Iraq. In a move defying the power players of the oil trade, Hussein's forces set fire to oil fields in Kuwait, filling the air with thick black smoke. He also had Kuwaiti oil dumped into the Persian Gulf. A greasy film spread across the water.

Hussein sent his troops to the Saudi border between Kuwait and Saudi Arabia. Iraqi soldiers stood ready to invade Saudi Arabia.

King Fahd knew that his country and its oil fields were at great risk. He appealed to the United Nations, an international organization comprised of 191 member states that advocates for peace. Sometimes the UN also commissions the militaries of member countries to enforce international law. Fahd asked that the United Nations send troops to protect Saudi Arabia.

Troops arrived from 30 nations, including Middle Eastern countries. The overwhelming bulk of protective forces, though, came from the United States. In a famous mission codenamed Operation Desert Shield, the U.S. sent about 400,000 soldiers to bolster

Saudi Arabia's foreign minister, Saud al-Faisal, meets with U.S. President George W. Bush on September 20, 2001, shortly after terrorist attacks destroyed the World Trade Center in New York City and damaged the Pentagon in Washington, D.C. Although Saudi leaders, including Crown Prince Abdullah, promised Saudi Arabia's full cooperation in the U.S.-led war on terrorism, some observers feel the country has not done enough to crack down on radical fundamentalists. In June 2002, Saudi officials arrested 13 men who were suspected of being part of the al-Qaeda terrorist network.

Saudi Arabia against Iraq. For many months, the American and other foreign troops remained in Saudi Arabia to deter Hussein from further advances. Both Saudi Arabia and the West repeatedly told Hussein to withdraw from Kuwait. Hussein refused.

In January 1991, the United States led a military campaign to drive Iraqi troops out of Kuwait. This second mission was code named Operation Desert Storm, and it was fast and aggressive. In a very brief time, Kuwait was free. Saudi Arabia was no longer directly threatened by an Iraqi invasion.

In the years following Operation Desert Storm, King Fahd suffered a number of health problems. In 1995, after Fahd spent time in the hospital, his brother, Crown Prince Abdullah, began to take on some of the king's duties. Although Fahd remained the official king, since 2000 Abdullah has been widely recognized as the *de facto* ruler of Saudi Arabia.

His leadership came at a crucial time in world affairs. On September 11, 2001, a group of terrorists launched unprecedented attacks against major U.S. public targets. Many of the terrorists, including their leader, Osama bin Laden, were Saudi citizens. Crown Prince Abdullah decried the attackers as renegades who should be punished.

Abdullah's statements, though, also included complaints about Israel's conduct toward the Palestinians. Clearly, issues were far from settled in the Middle East. And the unfolding history of Saudi Arabia still has matters that are yet to be resolved.

A large petrochemical facility in Saudi Arabia. Since the 1970s the country has been the largest producer and exporter of oil in the world. Saudi Aramco, the national oil company, has nine modern refineries to process the oil, so that millions of barrels can be exported each day.

Politics, Religion and the Economy

When Abd al-Aziz ibn Saud first founded his new country in 1932, he was very clear on one particular point: the nation would be based on the teachings of Islam. Abd al-Aziz also declared that the new country would be a kingdom. All future rulers would descend from Abd al-Aziz' own family, the House of Saud.

On the surface, neither of these declarations seems unusual. Other countries in today's Middle East are also tied closely to Islam, and a monarchy is a time-honored form of government. On closer inspection, though, it becomes clear that Saudi Arabia has managed to combine its connection to Islam with its monarchy in such a way as to form a government that is truly unique.

GOVERNMENT

In most other nations, power within a country is distributed through various channels. In the United States, for example, the government has three branches—judicial, legislative, and executive—that counterbalance one another, so that power is not concentrated in one single area. Additionally, adult citizens have the right to vote. American voters choose their own elected officials and help decide many laws and policies.

In Saudi Arabia, people do not vote. They do not participate in elections to choose their own rulers. Male citizens can attend weekly public meetings, known as **majlis**, to discuss their concerns with government officials. But the officials are not bound to act on

Saudi Arabia is far from a democracy—the king holds all power. However, Saudi leaders have traditionally given their people an opportunity to discuss government affairs. (Bottom) King Abd al-Aziz meets with subjects at a formal *majlis*, 1950s. (Left) A meeting of the *Majlis al-Shura* (Consultative Council), an advisory board that offers suggestions on domestic issues to the king.

The Arabic script on the flag of Saudi Arabia is the *Shahada*, the declaration of Muslim faith. It means: "There is no god but Allah, and Muhammad is His Prophet." Green is a traditional color of Islam.

any suggestions or complaints. Power remains strictly within the hands of government authorities, all of whom ultimately answer to the king. This appropriation of power makes the kingdom unique even among other apparently like-minded states.

Neighboring Jordan, for example, is a monarchy. But that country also has elected officials and a certain amount of power-sharing within the government. So, too, do monarchies throughout the West. In many modern Western monarchies, in fact, the king or queen performs mainly ceremonial functions, while the nation is actually run by elected officials. In Great Britain, for example, the head of state is the reigning monarch, but the head of government is the elected prime minister, who must work with Parliament to run the country.

In Saudi Arabia, the monarch is both the head of state and the head of government. He is both the king and the prime minister. He has so much authority that he is known as one of the world's last remaining absolute monarchs. This means that he is completely in charge of his country, and possesses an extremely broad range of powers.

In Saudi Arabia, the king approves all laws. He is in charge of the military, and selects all officers above the rank of lieutenant colonel. He chooses his country's foreign ambassadors, and he sits at the head of his country's judicial system, having the final say on legal cases.

Obviously, even though he has absolute power, the king cannot run his entire nation single-handedly. In a way similar to how other world leaders operate, he receives help from a series of counselors, ministers, and lesser officials. He has a court system, a financial agency, and various boards and bureaus.

The most visible government organization in Saudi Arabia is the Council of Ministers. This is a group of powerful officials who oversee important national matters such as foreign trade, military operations, and education. There are 20 ministries in all.

The king personally chooses the minister for each of the 20 agencies. The ministers in charge of the four most important bureaus—defense, foreign affairs, interior, and public works—traditionally belong to the king's own family, the House of Saud. In lesser ministries, many of the deputy ministers also belong to the royal family. The Council of Ministers has a certain measure of authority, but even so, that power is closely regulated. The king has final approval over any of the Council's rules or decrees.

In addition to the Council of Ministers, the king also has the Consultative Council to advise him on matters of national importance. The council has no authority to enact laws or change existing regulations; it only gives advice. There are 60 members on the council, each of whom the king personally chooses. Each member is appointed to a four-year renewable term of service.

On the local level, the country is divided into 13 provinces. Each province is run by its own provincial council, consisting of a governor and his deputy, plus at least 10 appointed citizens. Each provisional council handles the various plans and projects of its own area. Again, the king chooses the governors and deputy governors.

The Saudi Arabian king has yet another unique power: he can choose his own successor. In traditional monarchies, the crown passes down from the king or queen to the eldest son or daughter. In Saudi Arabia, though, the king selects the next ruler. The ruler is never a female, but is always a close male relative, such as a son, grandson, or brother. The successor is known as the Crown Prince.

Ultimately, the Crown Prince becomes king when the old monarch dies or is unable to rule. In the late 1990s, for example, King Fahd became increasingly weakened by various health problems. Crown Prince Abdullah began assuming more and more responsibilities of the monarchy, until by 2002 he was effectively in charge of the country.

The Economy of Saudi Arabia

Gross domestic product (GDP*): $173 billion

GDP per capita: $7,230

Inflation: 1.7%

Natural resources: petroleum, natural gas, iron ore, gold, copper (2000 est.)

Agriculture (7% of GDP): date palms and other fruits, grains, vegetables

Industry (48% of GDP): oil and oil byproducts (jet fuel, petroleum gas, kerosene), utilities, cement, crude steel (2000 est.)

Services (45% of GDP): government services, banking, insurance, consulting, other (2000 est.)

Foreign trade:

   Imports—$66.9 billion: petroleum and petroleum products

   Exports—$29.7 billion: machinery and equipment, foodstuffs, chemicals, motor vehicles, textiles

Currency exchange rate: 3.7450 Saudi riyals = $1 U.S. (2003)

*GDP, or gross domestic product, is the total value of goods and services produced in a country annually.
All figures are 2001 estimates unless otherwise noted.
Sources: CIA World Factbook, 2002; World Bank.

RELIGION AND GOVERNMENT

In addition to his political role as king and prime minister, the Saudi king also has an important religious function: he is the Custodian of the Two Holy Mosques. This title refers to the mosques at Mecca and Medina, which are the two most revered sites of Islam—not just in Saudi Arabia, but also throughout the Muslim world. Every year, millions of Muslims come from all over the world to worship at the mosques. The Council of Ministers even has a special ministry devoted to religious pilgrimages.

The Saudi king's religious title, Custodian of the Two Holy Mosques, carries a powerful message: the Saudi king and his nation play a key role in the Islamic world's ongoing observance of religious practice. But if Saudi Arabia has a special

Saudi men pray at a small mosque in Jidda. Saudi Arabia plays an important role as the country that contains the holiest sites of Islam.

place in the world of Islam, so too does Islam play a unique part in the workings of Saudi Arabia.

It is difficult at first for Westerners to understand the relationship between religion and government in Saudi Arabia. In America, in particular, people are accustomed to religious freedom.

> **Saudi Arabia produces the largest date crop in the world. Each year, the kingdom donates tens of thousands of tons of dates to countries that need food.**

Most governments of the world cannot tell their citizens where or how to pray, or even if they must pray at all. Here, the churches and the government are officially independent of one another, a principle called the separation of church and state. It is so rooted a tenet in our culture that it is often taken for granted.

The situation is completely the opposite in Saudi Arabia, where the government and religion are closely intertwined. Only in Iran, where Islamic religious leaders participate directly in government, does religion play a more important role in the workings of a Middle Eastern government.

The role of government is set forth in the Saudi Arabian Basic Law of Government. Article One states the following:

> The Kingdom of Saudi Arabia is a sovereign Arab Islamic state with Islam as its religion; God's Book and the Sunna of His Prophet, God's prayers and peace be upon him, are its constitution, Arabic is its language and Riyadh is its capital.

This means that in Saudi Arabia, the most fundamental document of government, the constitution, is based on the Qur'an. The government's rules and regulations are set forth in the *Sunna*, which is derived from the *Hadith*, a collection of sayings and teachings of the prophet Muhammad. The country's laws are provided by Islamic *Sharia*, or religious law.

The Basic Law of Government also states citizens must pay allegiance to the king in accordance with the Qur'an, and that families must be raised on the basis of the Islamic faith. In the Council of Ministers, members cannot assume their posts until they swear to be loyal first to their religion, and then to king and country. According to a number of articles in the Basic Law of Government, society itself is based on Islamic values. In order to gain more insight into the government of Saudi Arabia, then, it is important to examine the workings of Islam.

AN OVERVIEW OF ISLAM

Like Judaism and Christianity, Islam is monotheistic, meaning it proclaims only one God. Muslims respect some of the same important biblical figures that are found in Judaism and Christianity: they trace their ancestry to Abraham, and believe Moses and Jesus were inspired by the word of God. However, they do not accept the Christian belief that Jesus was divine, or that he was the Son of God. They consider him a prophet, bringing a divine message from God.

Muslims believe that the final revelations from God were given to their own prophet, Muhammad. They also believe that no more prophets, messiahs, or saviors will follow Muhammad.

The Muslim faith is contained in a single statement, the *Shahada*, which means "testimony." The testimony states: "There is no god but Allah, and Muhammad is His Prophet." *Allah* is the Arabic word for God.

Islam has five basic rules called the Five Pillars. The first is to believe and recite the *Shahada*. The other four pillars are as follows:

Salat (prayer): Muslims pray five times each day. The prayers are said at sunrise, noon, mid-afternoon, sunset, and evening. A special announcer, called a *muezzin*, cries out the prayer times to the community; those too far away to hear the *muezzin* simply pray at the proper time.

Zakat (almsgiving): Similar to the Judeo-Christian concept of tithing, *Zakat* asks that Muslims contribute a portion of their personal wealth to the community.

Sawm (fasting): In order seek a deeper understanding of God, Muslims maintain strict dietary rules during the month of Ramadan. This is the Islamic calendar's ninth month, the month in which Muslims believe that Muhammad received his revelations. During Ramadan, Muslims may not eat or drink between sunrise and sunset. Certain people, including pregnant women and young children, are excused from the strict fast.

Hajj (the pilgrimage to Mecca): If they are financially and physically capable, Muslims are required to travel to Mecca at least once in their lifetimes. Mecca is revered as the birthplace of both Islam and Muhammad. Every year, millions of Muslims from all over the world embark on the annual hajj. They converge on their holy city to worship during the Islamic calendar's twelfth month. They also often visit Medina, a highly revered site where Muhammad lived.

Most Muslims—about 85 percent of the worldwide population—follow a branch of the faith known as Sunni Islam. People who practice Sunni believe that they follow the true teachings of Muhammad. Within the Sunni division is the strict, conservative Wahhabi sect of Islam. Wahhabism is the dominant form of the religion practiced in Saudi Arabia today, as 90 to 95 percent of the country's population follows Wahhabi Islam.

Saudi Arabia is also home to a small community of Muslims who follow Shia Islam, the minority branch of the faith. Shiites make up less than 15 percent of the worldwide Islamic population, although some Middle Eastern states, like Iran, Bahrain, Iraq, and Lebanon, have Shiite majorities. In Saudi Arabia, between 5 and 10 percent of the population follows Shia Islam. Shiites are concentrated mainly in the Eastern Province.

ISLAM AND THE LAW

In Saudi Arabia, religion is more than a personal system of belief. *Sharia* applies to all areas of life in Saudi Arabia, including those that traditionally are not governed by laws in the West. In the West, for example, people are in many situations required to dress according to established standards of decency. Under those standards, people are basically free to choose their own style of clothing. Not so in Saudi Arabia, where *Sharia* requires modesty. There is a rigid standard of dress, particularly for women.

In Saudi Arabia, the law requires women to cover their bodies when they are in public. Women must wear long, flowing gowns. The gowns, known as **abayahs**, must be solid black, with no decorations. They cover the entire body, including the face, from head to toe. They conceal so much, in fact, that it is impossible for an observer to tell whether a woman beneath an *abayah* is young or old, thin or plump. Even in the heat of summer, all women must wear the thick, black gowns.

The law concerning *abayahs* is taken quite seriously. In May 2002, some Saudi Arabian government inspectors found that 82,000 newly manufactured *abayahs* did not meet Islamic standards. They were too clingy, or had decorations. Government officials seized the 82,000 offending *abayahs*. Other laws governing dress and conduct are treated with equal seriousness.

Islamic law is enforced in Saudi Arabia by a special group known as the Committees for the Propagation of Virtue and the Prevention of Vice. The committee agents are called the **Mutawin**. Their headquarters is in an office in Riyadh called the Royal Diwan, where the king also has his own headquarters.

The *Mutawin* have been part of the Wahhabi movement since its beginnings. In the early 1800s, the *Mutawin* acted as a form of religious police, physically forcing men to join in public prayer. Today, the *Mutawin* continue to enforce moral standards in Saudi Arabia. Their findings are taken quite seriously.

In 1991, for example, the *Mutawin* caught a Saudi man giving a female coworker a ride home from work. The act was forbidden; men and women who are not married or are not close relatives cannot be alone together. The woman, who came from a different country, was ordered to return to her native land. The man was beaten in public.

Punishments for other offenses are also harsh by Western standards. Thieves who are repeatedly caught stealing can have their right hands chopped off. People convicted of crimes related to alcohol can be whipped with a cane.

One of the most far-reaching set of laws in Saudi Arabia is that governing religious practice. All citizens must follow the teachings of Islam. The government is vigilant at keeping the country free of non-Muslim influences. Government inspectors routinely open mail from foreign countries and search for such items as Bibles or non-Islamic religious videos.

Theoretically, non-Muslims are allowed to practice their faiths in private, but no one is entirely sure what that means. In recent years, the U.S. State Department has reported several cases where non-Muslims have been punished for attending private religious services. In one instance, 16 Filipinos were arrested for attending a Christian prayer service. The Filipinos were later sent back to the Philippines. The State Department also reported that in 1998, an elderly man was attacked and killed because he performed a Shiite Muslim ritual in public.

CHANGING PERSPECTIVES OF ISLAM

Groups such as Amnesty International and the U.S. Department

Saudi Arabia has established a modern banking system. The country's currency is the Saudi riyal.

of State have expressed concern about these and other instances of religious intolerance. The groups have been particularly concerned about religious freedoms, and about the treatment of women in Saudi Arabia. Within Saudi Arabia, though, many people have a different perspective on how they live. Complaints about religious freedom and women's rights are viewed as being Western notions that have no place in the Muslim world.

In recent years, particularly after the Persian Gulf War, people in Saudi Arabia have expressed different views on how they should live their lives. Some have wanted to be more open to Western ideas. Others have chosen to adhere more closely to their interpretation of Islamic law. In the early 1990s, for example, Saudi Arabian radio and television stations began to increase their religious programming. Newspapers had more articles about religion. This religious revivalism spread in ways that surprised people in the West. In the United States and Great Britain, for example, educated young women traditionally have worked throughout history to obtain greater freedoms for women. During the revival of the 1990s, however, many educated young women covered their bodies even more thoroughly than the law already required.

Religion has been both a backbone and a challenge to the Saudi nation, as the country has worked to balance a conservative outlook against an economy that gives it great prominence in world affairs.

ECONOMY

Before Saudi Arabia became a country, the region had no unified economy. In the Hejaz, the western province, the economy was based on a combination of agriculture, trade, and income from the annual hajj. In the Eastern Province, the economy was based mainly on the date crop.

The new nation's fortunes—and its economy—changed drastically in the 1930s, as a result of two significant factors. The first was the discovery of oil in the Arabian Peninsula. The second was the large European demands for that oil. European countries, rebuilding from the devastation of World War II, needed large quantities of oil to fuel new projects and developments, many of which had recently replaced coal-fired with oil-fired fuel systems. Suddenly, Saudi Arabia had a product that was in high demand. Almost

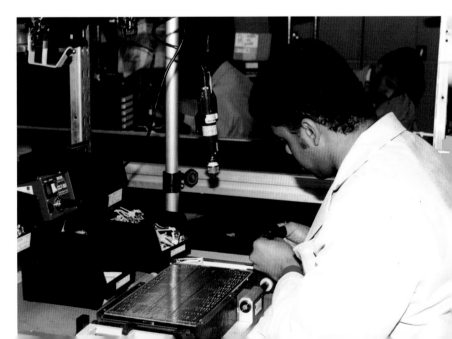

A technician works on a circuit board. Saudi Arabian companies manufacture computer components and other high-tech products.

overnight, the new kingdom became exceptionally wealthy.

Abd al-Aziz knew that in order for his country to become truly one nation, it had to be unified by more than just its name. There had to be physical connections uniting the provinces separated by vast expanses of desert. Put simply, the country had to function. Abd al-Aziz thus decided to spend huge sums of money on modernization projects that dealt with roads, hospitals, schools, transportation, agriculture, and industry.

Over the years, as Western nations needed more and more oil, money continued to flow into Saudi Arabia. By the 1980s, however, countries found oil in plentiful supply all over the world, and oil prices fell. Yet the Saudi Arabian government still continued to spend in excess. In 1982, even the massive income from international oil sales was not enough to pay the country's debts. In 1987, Saudi Arabia began to borrow money.

A Saudi craftsman shows off some of his wares.

The 1990s brought even more economic complications. In 1990–91, Saudi Arabia spent about $55 billion on the Gulf War. The country managed to pay off its debts to other nations by 1995, but then borrowed $4.3 billion in order to buy aircraft. At the end of the decade, the government's internal debts (money owed within the country) reached $130 billion, more than 90 percent of the **gross domestic product**, a standard that measures a country's output of goods and services.

Another factor impacting the Saudi Arabian economy was the makeup of the workforce. A large percentage of the labor force of Saudi Arabia came from—and still come from—foreign countries. One study from 2000 concluded that the foreign workforce in Saudi Arabia consisted of some 7.2 million people, nearly 47 percent of the Saudi population. These workers essentially took the jobs of native Saudis, keeping the unemployment rate high.

The government developed a number of measures to put its economy back on track. It raised the cost of utilities such as electricity and water. It cut back on government spending. International oil prices went up, bringing added revenue. Additionally, the government worked to develop sources of income beyond the oil industry, and aggressively worked to reduce the imbalance of foreign workers to native workers.

Today, the Saudi Arabian economy is still centered on the oil industry. More than 90 percent of the nation's income stems from oil and petroleum products. But Saudi Arabia also produces cement, electrical appliances, and crude steel and other metal goods. The country that once depended heavily on its date crop and on income from the hajj is also active in commercial banking and other non-oil related ventures.

In a short period of time, this young nation has changed greatly. But remnants of the ancient culture live on, in the hearts of the Arab people.

The minarets of the Great Mosque of Mecca. Special announcers called *muezzins* cry out from these towers before each of the day's prayer meetings.

The People

Long before King Abd al-Aziz envisioned his desert kingdom, the Arabian Peninsula was sparsely populated by nomadic people known as bedouins. Some bedouins still roam the deserts of Saudi Arabia—not atop camels, but from behind the wheels of their sturdy sport utility vehicles. For the most part, though, the hardy tribespeople and their descendants are well settled. Arabs no longer live in tents in the desert. They live in towns and cities, in modern homes, with access to cars and public transportation. But much of their character and customs still trace back to an earlier day, when life was far different.

THE ARAB HORSE

One of the most romantic themes of the Arab past is the bedouins' special history with their magnificent horses. Even in America, people who know about horses revere the legend of the Arab horse. Stunningly beautiful but also remarkably tough, the Arab horse was so close to its bedouin master that individual animals shared their owners' food and water. Some actually slept in their masters' tents. The horses became accustomed to the ways of humans, and learned to serve them well, particularly in warfare.

During raids against rival tribes, the quick Arab horses galloped headlong over vast stretches of thick sand, enabling their riders to swoop in to battle and then quickly out again. The favored war animal, the Arab mare, knew to remain silent during raids, so as not to alert the enemy. The mares were so valued that they were never sold. The only way a mare would trade hands was if she were stolen or given as a gift.

In the seventh century, the prophet Muhammad knew that he would have to fight many battles to establish Islam. Muhammad realized that his soldiers would need hundreds of Arab horses, and the only available way to obtain more horses was to breed them.

Saudis wearing traditional dress and carrying ceremonial swords ride camels through the desert.

Because of the desert terrain of the Arabian Peninsula, the country is sparsely populated. Pockets of population can be found along the Red Sea and Persian Gulf, and around the country's capital at Riyadh.

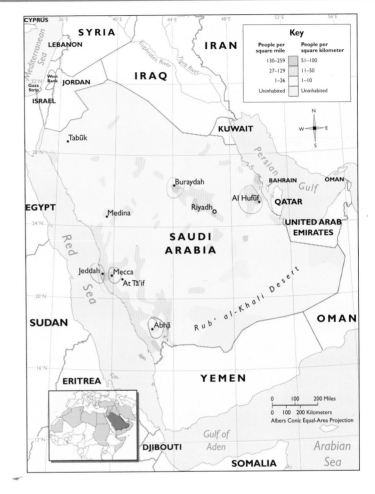

The period between when a foal is conceived to when it is ready to be ridden is about three years. With an eye to the future, Muhammad insisted that his followers increase their efforts to breed horses. Many people in the West acknowledge Muhammad for helping to create a tough and loyal strain of horse that survives to this day.

Muhammad is also credited for encouraging the humane treatment of these special animals. He said that Allah treasured the horse because he created it himself. The prophet also declared that anyone who treated the horse well would be rewarded in the afterlife. Even the Qur'an spoke well of the horse, and said that no evil spirit would enter a tent that contained a purebred Arab horse.

Today, you will not find horses sleeping in their masters' homes in Saudi Arabia. As in most of the rest of the world, the horse is no longer an essential part of daily life. But throughout the desert kingdom, the Arab horse continues to surface as a cultural theme in sports, literature, and art. One painting by Prince Khaled al-Faisal, an accomplished artist as well as a royal figure, is a charming scene of a bedouin and his horse. In the painting, the horse has a sweet expression on its face, and seems devoted to its master.

The People of Saudi Arabia

Population: 25,513,330 (July 2002 est.)
Ethnic groups: Arab 90%, Afro-Asian 10%
Religions: Muslim 100%
Language: Arabic
Age structure:
0–14 years: 42.4%
15–64 years: 54.8%
65 years and over: 2.8%
Population growth rate: 3.27%
Birth rate: 37.25 births/1,000 population
Death rate: 5.86 deaths/1,000 population
Infant mortality rate: 49.59 deaths/1,000 live births
Life expectancy at birth:
total population: 68.4 years
males: 66.7 years
females: 70.2 years
Total fertility rate: 6.21 children born/woman
Literacy (age 15 and older): 78%

All figures are 2002 estimates.
Source: CIA World Factbook, 2002

THE SAUDI ARABIAN HOME

Many Saudi traditions basically remain unchanged; others survive, though with a modern twist. Traditions involving family and the home remain central to life in Saudi Arabia. In earlier days, Arab families often visited their relatives' tents, or welcomed visitors themselves. Families also liked to spend their free time together in the open—in the desert, the mountains, or at sea. Today, Arab families still spend considerable time together.

Arab homes tend to have open, airy rooms that are marked by distinctive arches and spire-shaped doorways. These architectural shapes date back to earlier times, and are similar to those found on mosques and other public buildings. The openness in the homes allows air to circulate and help cool the household.

Saudi families have modern-style tables for their meals. On special occasions, though, meals are laid out in the traditional manner, with the food served on a large cloth placed on the floor. The family then sits or squats around the edges of the cloth and selects from a variety of foods placed in the center.

The home is also used to entertain visitors. Most homes have an area called the *majlis*, a gathering spot for friends and guests. Chairs or pillows are set low to the ground, where Arabs sometimes still squat in the traditional manner.

Arabs have special traditions for making their guests feel welcome. Saudi hosts show their appreciation of their guests by burning incense in their honor. They also use bottled rosewater as a room freshener or as a special flavor to desserts. As in the West, Saudi hosts serve coffee to their guests. Arab coffee is ground with an aromatic spice known as cardamom. Some Arabs say that just the smell of cardamom makes them feel welcome. The spiced coffee is served in small, dainty cups, with little treats on the side. Hosts

A family sits down to a traditional dinner in Saudi Arabia.

also often serve one of Saudi Arabia's most favorite treats—sweetened dates.

FASHION

In general, Saudi women are very fashion-conscious. It is true that when women go out in public, they are covered by their *abayahs*. But beneath their robes, they wear beautiful clothing. Their outfits are colorful and dramatic, with elaborate embroidery or long, flowing sleeves and headscarves.

Saudi women also are fond of jewelry. Some of their jewels follow the modern style of using diamonds and other precious stones. But women also wear the intricate designs that were first created centuries ago by bedouin craftsmen.

The jewelry itself has an interesting history. The patterns and styles date back for centuries, to ancient times, when craftsmen prided themselves on creating elaborate designs from silver. Bedouin jewelry is one of the most popular kinds. To make it, the metal is heated over fire to make it pliable, or soft. Then it is fashioned into narrow threads that are woven into chain mail, or mesh. The finished pieces are large and dramatic, and are affixed with jangling coins or miniature bells. Sometimes, the larger sections are embossed with elegant Arabic writing.

The jewelry sometimes contains different stones that are believed to have special powers over those who wear them. Coral bestows wisdom, agate softens the personality of whoever wears it by making them more agreeable. Turquoise, one of the most popular gems and a fashionable American stone, calms the emotions and reduces stress.

Bedouin jewelry—which comes in necklaces, anklets, bracelets, and rings—once played a role in wedding tradition. A young man would pay his future father-in-law a dowry, or bride-price. The bride's father would use part of that money to buy jewelry for the young bride. The jewelry was hers to keep, and to sell if she ever became impoverished. Now, the jewelry is still prized for its beauty, and adds much to what a woman wears under the *abayah* or in the privacy of her home.

Clothing for Saudi men is far less decorative or varied. They wear a long, floor-length robe known as a *thobe*. The *thobe* looks much like a long shirt, with a collar and cuffs. It is almost always white. On their heads, men wear a three-part covering. The first part is a *kuffiyah*, or skullcap. Over the *kuffiyah*, men wear a large folded cloth called a *ghutra*. The *ghutra* is either white or checkered

Saudi women wear black *abayahs* and cover their faces in public, or when they are in the presence of men who are not members of their family. This is required by Islamic law in Saudi Arabia. Beneath their *abayahs*, however, women often wear brightly colored clothing and ornate jewelry.

with red and white. It is fastened into place with a black woolen coil called an igal. Sometimes Saudi men wear an additional cloak, called a *bisht* or *mishlah*, on top of the *thobe*. The cloak is usually light beige or black, and is reserved for cool weather, or for formal settings.

Saudi men's clothing is based on old bedouin traditions. Among nomads, the outer robes also served as blankets for sleeping in the desert. The woolen igal was originally a halter used at night on camels. In the day, it was wrapped around a man's head. There, it secured in place the *ghutra* that helped ward off the harsh rays of the intense desert sun.

In the past, Arab men wore styles that were more colorful and elaborate than those seen today. Different regions produced brightly colored robes and head wrappings of uniquely patterned styles. Today, those varied styles are mostly seen at cultural events that are held to preserve the fading traditions.

JENADRIYAH FESTIVAL

One of the most popular of those events is the Jenadriyah National Culture and Heritage Festival. This event is held every January just outside Riyadh in the city of Jenadriyah, which was built solely for the purpose of holding the festival.

The yearly festival lasts for two weeks. Men and women do not attend the festival together, so some days are set aside only for men to attend; the others day are reserved for the women. The festival showcases traditional music, dance, and crafts. It allows visitors to tour traditional **souqs**, or markets, and to look at replicas of old mud forts and historic towns.

Opening the festival every year is a performance of the Ardha, an ancient sword dance that is also the Saudi Arabian national dance. Another very popular event is the traditional camel race, which draws thousands of fans from all over the region. Westerners who attend the races are amazed to see that the jockeys are actually young boys, chosen for their small stature and their ability to cling to the backs of the giant, lumbering beasts.

The little jockeys are well paid for their skill. Winners reportedly can earn as much as $10,000 in a three-month racing season that takes them beyond the Jenadriyah festival. Race prizes can include more than just cash. Winners at Jenadriyah have been awarded pickup trucks or other types of sand-skimming sport utility vehicles. Unlike Western countries, Saudi Arabia does not allow people to gamble at racetracks. But the fast-moving camel races, held both in the open desert and on the confined track, receive a noisy, ecstatic response from the crowds.

STORYTELLING AND CALLIGRAPHY

The festival also features the much more sedate, but also time-honored, traditions of Arabic storytelling and poetry. In ancient times, Arabs placed great value on storytellers and poets. Poetic minstrels memorized thousands of lines of poetry, and traveled from place to place, reciting lengthy epics. Along with having a beautiful sound, these poems also told old stories and revealed histories of distant eras. The poems and poets played—and at the Jenadriyah festival, still play—a special role in preserving the history, folklore, and traditions of the Arab people.

Other histories and religious works were preserved in writing. Now, a renewed interest in old writings has brought about a revival in another Arab tradition, the art of calligraphy.

Calligraphy is a highly decorative form of handwriting. In calligraphy, individual letters of the alphabet have elaborate shape, and are carefully drawn for artistic effect. In Saudi Arabia, calligraphy appears on paper, but also on glass, ceramics, textiles, metal work, and the walls of mosques and other buildings. The Saudi government helps to sponsor the preservation of this tradition. Calligraphy com-

Elementary school students participate in an art class. Education is an important part of life in Saudi Arabia.

petitions are held throughout Saudi Arabia. Students are encouraged to learn the age-old art form.

EDUCATION

Not all Saudi culture is rooted in ancient practice. The education system, for instance, is younger than the kingdom itself. In earlier times, formal education did not exist. Bedouin children did not attend schools as we know them, but instead were taught by their own families. Towns and villages had special elementary schools known as *kuttab*, where young children were taught to recite verses from the Qur'an. The classes were usually run by a local mosque, or were taught in the home. Many children—girls in particular—never did learn to read or write.

When Abd al-Aziz founded his kingdom in 1932, he acknowledged the importance of education. Without education, the people would lack the knowledge and the skills that were needed to build a modern country. At first, schools were organized only for boys. Girls were raised to be wives, mothers, and homemakers, with teaching and nursing the only available professions. Now, there are also schools for girls.

Students in Saudi Arabia attend kindergarten, followed by six years of primary school, three years of intermediate school, and three years of high school. At the high school level, students attend either academic school, where they focus on arts and sciences, or vocational school to learn a trade. All schools focus on the teachings of Islam, and all are under the management of the clergy.

For many years, students who wanted to study advanced subjects at a university had to travel abroad. Every year, young Saudi high school graduates departed for large universities in Great Britain, the United States, or other countries. The Saudi government paid for its young people to study in foreign countries. In addition to paying the tuition, the government provided money for lodging, food, and transportation.

Women could study in other countries only if a husband or a close male relative went along to guard them. Men who wanted to study overseas were encouraged to get married first, and to bring their wives and children with them. The Saudi government used this approach with its male students because it worried that they would become confused or corrupted by non-Islamic societies.

In 1984, about 10,000 Saudi students were enrolled at foreign universities. Now, that number is much smaller. Most students remain within Saudi Arabia to study at large universities that have sprung up in various cities throughout the country.

King Faisal University, which has campuses in the cities of Ad Dammam and Al Hufuf, is known for its programs in medicine and veterinary science. The Islamic University of Medina teaches Islamic law and Arab literature, among other subjects. King Saud

University, in the capital city of Riyadh, offers an array of special-
ties, from agriculture through engineering.

SPORTS

There have been other modern developments in the world of
Saudi Arabian sports. In recent years, the Saudi government has
built high quality sports facilities to accommodate popular international events such as soccer, volleyball, and basketball. The
government is in the process of building a series of vast sports
complexes, each called Sports City, at various sites throughout
the kingdom. Each Sports City features large indoor and outdoor
stadiums, plus Olympic-sized swimming pools and an assortment
of game courts and conference halls. The King Fahd Stadium in
Riyadh holds thousands of spectators.

Even though modern sports are gaining popularity, Saudis still

Soccer is a popular sport,
particularly among young
Saudis.

enjoy the sporting events that date back to ancient times, including camel racing, dog racing, and falconry. Ancient dog racers in Saudi Arabia used one of the world's oldest domesticated dogs, the Saluki, which comes from southern Arabia. Modern Arabs still breed and race these elegant dogs. Falconry, a sport in which trained birds and their handlers take part in hunting-type competitions, is especially popular among wealthy Arabs.

As much as Saudi Arabia has entered the modern world by adapting old customs to modern life, by keeping its traditions it has staked out a special place for itself in an ever-growing world culture. The noble Arab horse, once the pride of the desert nomads, has captured the imagination of horse lovers the world over. Today, hundreds of thousands of Arab horses are in the United States alone. In fact, the first Arabian horse in America was owned by the first U.S. president himself, George Washington.

Such a far reach for the far-flung bedouin of the desert! And an interesting beginning for Saudi Arabia's relationships with nations far beyond its boundaries.

The traditional architecture of this mosque in Jidda stands in contrast to the newer office buildings behind it.

Communities

Few Westerners can describe a typical community in Saudi Arabia. Unlike many other countries throughout the world, Saudi Arabia does not allow tourists or visitors to simply buy a plane ticket and make hotel reservations. Nor does the desert kingdom allow people to apply for a tourist visa, a document that permits entry for a limited period of time.

A certain number of foreigners, many of whom are in the oil industry, live in Saudi Arabia because they work for companies that conduct business there. But foreigners wishing to visit Saudi Arabia must have a special sponsor—a Saudi citizen who personally issues an invitation. Even then, not all people who have a sponsor are allowed to visit the country. And those who are allowed in are not always assured that they may stay.

In 2001, for example, an American writer was sponsored to visit Saudi Arabia. After a long journey, the writer arrived at the airport in Riyadh. Instead of being allowed to proceed to his hotel, though, the writer was taken aside for a discussion with government officials. The officials said that someone had found an "unfavorable" article the writer had written about Saudi Arabia some 15 years earlier. After many long hours of talks, and with the help of the writer's sponsor, the writer was allowed to remain in the country. With visits so carefully controlled, it is no wonder that so few non-Saudis can describe firsthand the cities of Saudi Arabia.

Westerners may be surprised, then, to learn what cities are really like in the desert kingdom. As in the West, they are varied. Just as Miami is different from Minneapolis, so, too, are the cities of Saudi Arabia different from one another. True, there is a national culture that is strong throughout the country, but each place has its own unique look and feel.

Certain large Saudi cities, when seen from a far distance, look very much like similarly sized cities in the United States. On closer inspection, though, a visitor finds that those seemingly Western-style cities are distinctly Arab.

JIDDA

Jidda (sometimes spelled *Jeddah*, or *Jiddah*) is one Saudi Arabian city with a deceptively Western appearance. The largest city on the Red Sea coast, Jidda is the second-largest city in the kingdom. Its name means "Ancestor of Women." At one time, it was believed that Jidda was the site of Eve's tomb.

Famed for being open, friendly, and glamorous, Jidda is known as the Paris of Arabia. The sparkling city is also an important center for business and industry. It is one of the busiest seaports in the entire region.

When viewed from the air, Jidda is a sprawling jumble of architecture. There are long, low buildings. There are also tall skyscrapers; cylindrical, or round, buildings festooned with dozens upon dozens of windows; and an intricate tangle of roads. Bridges span the various inlets of water. Huge ships float alongside massive docks that are stacked with shipping containers. Large cranes stand ready to load or unload cargo from around the world.

Jidda is home to a number of large trading companies and the country's national airline, Saudia. These companies employ a great many people who live in and around the city.

Jidda has become a popular tourist spot for Saudi Arabians living elsewhere. There are many hotels, restaurants, and shopping malls. There are also many features that set it apart from any other city in the world. Just as New York has its distinctive Statue of Liberty, and Paris has its unique Eiffel Tower, Jidda has a vast open-air plaza, the Corniche.

The Corniche contains an open-air sculpture garden, with more than 400 eye-catching, oversized creations. One work resembles a large fluted-edge shell, or petal; another captures the look of birds in flight. The popular plaza also has street vendors and carnivals with games and rides for thrill-seekers. Equally as impressive as the Corniche is the enormous decorative fountain located near the Al Salam Palace that shoots a stream of water high into the air. It is said to be the highest fountain in the world.

But even though Jidda, with its carnival rides and its collection of modern sculpture, leaves a very Western impression, its culture is nonetheless distinctly Islamic. The carnivals are divided into sections for men and for women. So, too, are the fast-food restaurants that place men in one area and families in another.

In addition to its modern shopping malls, Jidda also has traditional *souqs*. These are open-air markets where individual vendors set up stalls to sell their wares. Shopping malls in Jidda operate the way they do in the West, with fixed prices on every item. In the *souqs*, however, everyone expects to haggle, or bargain. In a haggling session, the seller first states a price, and the buyer responds by offering a much lower price. The seller then makes a counteroffer, lower than his original offer but higher than what the buyer offers to pay; and so on, until an agreement is reached.

RIYADH

A similar mix of old and new is also found in Saudi Arabia's capital city, Riyadh. The largest city in the kingdom, Riyadh is located in the country's central region, known as the Najd. With its roots reaching deeply into Islamic history, the Najd has a firm Islamic tradition throughout the region, with a strong emphasis

Riyadh, the capital of Saudi Arabia, is a fast-growing city with a population of more than 4.3 million.

placed on observance of the faith.

The royal dynasty itself first came to power around the year 1500 in the Najd, where members of the Al Saud family captured some date groves. The groves were located at Ad Diriyah, the Al Saud's original base (which was later destroyed by Ottoman-backed Egyptians).

In the late 19th century, the Al Saud's rival family, the Al Rashid, tried to establish their own stronghold in the Najd. Around 1865, the Al Rashid built the Masmakh Fortress at Riyadh, and by the 1870s they had forced the Al Saud into exile. In 1902, the Saudi leader Abd al-Aziz, then living in exile in Kuwait, attacked the Masmakh Fortress in an attempt to reclaim the Najd. From there, Abd al-Aziz captured Riyadh. He gradually took over the entire Najd and, eventually, the area that would become Saudi Arabia.

Today, the old Masmakh Fortress still remains in Riyadh, along with the many historic sites and museums in the city. Museum curators (people who take care of museum exhibits) have restored the dried mud fortress to its original condition. The fortress has a well that still provides water, a traditional *majlis* (a room where Arab hosts entertain guests), and a series of carved walls. The fortress is a popular tourist destination.

Just outside the town is a site that harks back to the earliest known activities in the Middle East: a huge camel market, which serves as a reminder of the old caravans that once traversed the inhospitable desert. Other sites within Riyadh include the Murabba Palace, where King Abd al-Aziz lived and worked, and a restored version of the Al-Thumairi Gate, one of nine gates that once led into Riyadh.

The city also has the Riyadh Museum and the King Saud University Museum. The two museums contain many artifacts, or cultural items, from earlier times. The Riyadh Museum contains exhibits of traditional Arab life, featuring items such as clothing, jewelry, cooking utensils, and musical instruments. The King Saud facility displays artifacts dating back to 300 B.C.

Even though Riyadh is deeply rooted in old Arabia, though, the city itself is very modern. That is of course partly because Riyadh plays such a central role in governing Saudi Arabia and in leading many of the surrounding Arab nations. But the city is also modern simply because much of it is new.

Riyadh has always been the nation's capital, but many of the kingdom's government offices and all of the foreign embassies originally were located far to the west, in Jidda. In the 1980s, all of the various ministries and embassies were moved to Riyadh.

The agencies and embassies needed buildings and office space. So the Saudi government launched a huge construction program. Vast sums of money were spent on erecting new embassies and offices, and on the supporting infrastructure, such as water, electricity, and telephone lines. Billions of dollars were spent on building an international airport at Riyadh. As a result of all this construction, Riyadh is filled with new, clean buildings and has a large, well-organized road system.

MECCA AND MEDINA

The yearly observation of hajj takes place in Saudi Arabia's third-largest city—Mecca. The holiest site of the Islamic world, Mecca has a population of about 1.3 million. It is where the prophet Muhammad was born in the sixth century. It is probably most famously known as the site of the Grand Mosque, an enormous house of worship that can hold more than 1 million people. The Grand Mosque houses a holy site known as the Ka'aba, which Muslims believe is a model of God's house in heaven. Muslims say that the Ka'aba was built by the first human, Adam, and then rebuilt by Abraham and his son Ishmael.

Anyone can look at Mecca from the hills of nearby Taif, the

nation's unofficial summer capital. But only Muslims are allowed to enter the city grounds of Mecca. Special checkpoints are stationed along the roads leading into the city, so that authorities may inspect the credentials of people traveling to Mecca. Non-Muslims are turned away.

Throughout the year, Muslims perform a ritual called the *Umrah*, which is an individual journey to Mecca. But another type of journey, the hajj, is performed only during the month of *Dhul Hijjah*, the last month of the Islamic year.

Every year, millions of Muslims come to Mecca from all over the world in order to perform the hajj. In 2002, more than 2 million pilgrims took part in the ritual. The government of Saudi Arabia goes to great lengths in order to accommodate pilgrims on the hajj. There is a government ministry devoted to hajj affairs and a special hajj air terminal at Jidda International Airport. The government erects far-reaching tent cities to accommodate the pilgrims; provides some 15,000 buses to transport the pilgrims to various stations; and donates food and water for the visitors.

The hajj is a major event that literally takes over Mecca and surrounding communities. Each year, the pilgrims begin to arrive in Saudi Arabia about two months before the onset of *Dhul Hijjah*. They stay in the various tent cities, or with relatives or friends in the kingdom.

When the hajj itself begins, the pilgrims begin to make their way to the Holy Mosque. They make for quite a sight: millions of men, dressed identically in long, white robes worn in a precise way, proceeding on foot across the roadways leading into Mecca.

Each day of the lengthy hajj has a precise purpose and ritual. There is a day for compiling a supply of water for the coming travels; a day for shaving the head; a day for entering the Grand Mosque; a day for symbolically stoning Satan; and much more.

One of the last acts of the hajj involves the ritual slaughter of

Jubail, a city on the Arabian Gulf, is the home of King Abd al-Aziz Naval Base, where U.S. troops are stationed in Saudi Arabia.

sacrificial sheep, which the Saudi government even helps with. The pilgrims buy their own sacrificial animals, but the kingdom makes sure that a selection is available. In 2002, the government supplied some 600,000 sheep, which were killed and then shipped to needy people around the world.

After visiting the Grand Mosque at Mecca, many pilgrims return to their homes. Others stay to visit the second holiest site in Islam, the Mosque of the Prophet at Medina.

Known for its profusion of date palms, Medina is the fourth-largest city in Saudi Arabia, and has a population of about 775,000 people. Located 308 miles (496 km) north of Mecca and slightly more inland, Medina was a lively center of literary and intellectual activity during the Middle Ages. It was once the setting for serious discussions on how to record and apply Islamic law. The city remains an intellectual center to this day. The Islamic University at Medina is known for its programs in Islamic culture and Arabic literature. It is a beautiful city, but, like Mecca, it is also closed to non-Muslims.

OTHER COMMUNITIES

Both Jidda and Riyadh are distinctive, large, well-known cities. They stand in contrast to Saudi Arabia's many lesser-known but fascinating smaller towns and settlements.

Al Hasa is Saudi Arabia's largest single oasis. An oasis is like an island of life set amid a barren desert. The most common image of an oasis is that of palm trees and a bubbling spring, surrounded by an endless stretch of sand. Al Hasa, located in the south of the kingdom's eastern region, is an oversized version of that image.

Enclosed on all sides by empty desert, Al Hasa sits atop a vast underground water supply. Fresh springwater bubbles to the surface, nourishing the vegetation that in other parts of the country could not even begin to sprout. Crops flourish as a result. The farms at Al Hasa are threatened, however, by violent windstorms that blow tons of sand across the oasis. In order to fend off the crop-destroying winds, the government has planted thick barriers of trees to keep out the sand and the wind.

Far to the southwest, near the border with Yemen, is a much smaller oasis: the remote settlement of Najran. An old caravan stop for frankincense traders, the Najran oasis has been utilized for some 4,000 years. Some say that Najran is now a stop for smugglers who ply their trade between Yemen and Saudi Arabia.

Although Najran is not well known outside Saudi Arabia, it is a popular national spot, with beautiful gardens, parks, and dramatic scenery. It has one of the kingdom's most interesting museums. Among its displays are photographs taken by Harold St. John Philby, the famed Arabist and former British spy.

The stretch of land that sits alongside the Persian Gulf is dotted with distinctive communities. Dhahran is home to a massive military base that was built in the 1940s by the United States Army Corps of Engineers. American troops were stationed in Dhahran both before and after the Persian Gulf War.

The town is also populated with a large number of expatriates (people who have left their own native countries to live in a foreign land). The expatriates are mainly people connected with the oil industry. There is an interesting community of people who once worked for the massive Saudi oil company, Aramco. Americans who have lived in Dhahran say that it is clean and remarkably safe. People have no need to worry about crime; they keep their doors unlocked and leave their keys in their cars.

Just outside Dhahran is Al Khobar, a busy industrial city populated by many fishermen. Al Khobar serves as a commercial center for the Eastern Province. The city has a reputation of being inhospitable to Westerners ever since the terrorist attack of 1996, in which Islamic fundamentalists bombed Khobar Towers, a U.S. military housing complex. Nineteen Americans were killed and more than 370 Americans and Saudis were injured in the attack.

To the east of Dhahran and Al Khobar is another culturally unique town, Al Qatif. Set on an oasis, Al Qatif is also home to large numbers of fishermen, as well as many of Saudi Arabia's Shiites, who practice the Shia faith. A form of Islam, Shia differs very much from the Sunni form that is practiced in Saudi Arabia. The Saudi government has said that Shiites may practice their faith in private. Sometimes the Saudi authorities do not actively seek out instances of Shiite observances in public. Other times, the authorities aggressively enforce laws excluding the public practice of Shia and other

King Fahd Port, located north of Jubail on the Red Sea, is at the center of a bustling industrial and commercial center.

non-Wahhabi forms of Islam. Despite the prohibitions on Shia Islam, it is still a visible influence on Al Qatif.

The most important Shiite celebration is Ashura. This holiday marks a battle that took place in Iraq in the year 680. Around October 20 of that year, a large army belonging to the Omayyad regime surrounded a small band of rebels at Kerbala, on the

Saudi dancers perform during a festival.

Euphrates River. All the rebels were killed, including Hussain, the prophet Muhammad's grandson. Shiites revere Hussain as the spiritual leader of Shia Islam.

During Ashura, Shiites retell the story of the massacre at Kerbala. Women and men weep openly. Men walk in large groups through the streets, sometimes beating themselves with chains in order to express sympathy for Hussain. The celebrations of Ashura are not particularly well known outside the Muslim community.

FESTIVALS

For all the differences that apply to the towns and cities in Saudi Arabia, there are of course factors that unite the nation into one large community. The most important of these is, of course, the Islamic faith.

Together, the people of Saudi Arabia celebrate Eid al-Adha, which marks the hajj. They observe the month of Ramadan, during which healthy adults join in a controlled fast. Also, they celebrate the end of the fast during the three-day feast of Eid al-Fitr.

The nation also has a non-religious holiday, National Day, which celebrates the founding of the kingdom on September 23, 1932. Americans might recognize similarities in this community celebration to their own national holiday, the Fourth of July. On the 70th celebration of National Day in 2002, Crown Prince Abdullah commemorated the kingdom's founder Abd al-Aziz in a speech to the Council of Ministers. He stated that 70 years after its birth, the Kingdom of Saudi Arabia is progressing along the path first set by its founder.

Two Apache helicopters pass over the desert of Saudi Arabia in January 1991, during Operation Desert Shield. Islamists have been angered by the continued presence of U.S. troops in Saudi Arabia. This has inspired terrorist attacks against American targets both in and out of the country.

Foreign Relations

*J*n late April 2002, United States press reports were filled with stories of a forthcoming visit from an intriguing foreigner. That foreigner was Saudi Arabia's Crown Prince Abdullah, who was coming to the United States to meet with President George W. Bush. The two would meet not at the White House, but at the president's ranch in Crawford, Texas. Despite the seemingly informal setting that the ranch offered, this was not a casual get-together. It was an important meeting between two powerful world leaders who hoped to work together on some major international issues.

For Crown Prince Abdullah, the meeting would not only impact his relations with the United States, but would also have an effect on his partnership with the nations of his own region. Both relationships are extremely important to Saudi Arabia.

Because of its role in the formation of Islam and the

preservation of the two Holy Mosques, Saudi Arabia has a unique identity within the Islamic world. Every Muslim around the world who hopes to make the religious pilgrimage (hajj) must come to Saudi Arabia. The kingdom takes pride in being able to accommodate, or at least handle, the millions of pilgrims.

In the past, due to the great volume of the visitors, many pilgrims have suffered disasters such as stampedes and large-scale fires. Other Muslim states have criticized Saudi Arabia for not preventing the incidents. Now, Saudi Arabia goes to great lengths to ensure that the hajj operates smoothly and peacefully. In this and in other ways, Saudi Arabia is a leader among other Muslim nations, but it must work to maintain the respect and cooperation of its neighbors.

SAUDI ARABIA AND OPEC

Because of its position as a major source of the world's oil supply, Saudi Arabia has to maintain a good working relationship with its buyers around the world, particularly those in the United States and Europe. Although this might seem to place the kingdom in a position of great power because it has something the rest of the world really needs, Saudi Arabia has needs of its own. It is highly dependent on the United States for national defense, for example.

At times, the desert kingdom has had to make difficult choices and compromises in order to maintain good relations both with its neighbors in the Middle East and its associates in the West. Many of these compromises have involved the production and sale of oil.

In 1960, Saudi Arabia helped form a group that was designed to protect the interests of oil-producing nations. The group, named the Organization of Petroleum Exporting Countries (OPEC), consisted of Saudi Arabia, Iran, Iraq, Kuwait, and Venezuela. Over the years, eight additional countries joined the group: Algeria, Ecuador, Gabon, Indonesia, Libya, Nigeria, Qatar, and the United Arab Emirates.

The purpose of OPEC was to establish a single set of policies for all members to use with the sale of oil. Additionally, OPEC intended to stabilize oil prices. In that way, no country would set a very low price on its oil while another country used a far higher one. In practice, OPEC has expanded its reach by in effect becoming an instrument of foreign policy. The events following the October 1973 Arab-Israeli war, waged between Israel and two neighboring countries, are an illustrative example of OPEC's influence.

In 1973, Syria and Egypt launched an attack on Israel. The two Arab countries wanted to force Israel to withdraw from disputed territories, and to recognize certain rights of the Palestinian people. The attack came during Yom Kippur, the most holy Jewish holiday.

Saudi Arabia and other Arab nations supported Syria and Egypt. The world—already shocked by the attack—was even more stunned when the Soviet Union, the huge Communist superpower, joined in the fray. Although the Soviets did not send an army to the Middle

Crown Prince Abdullah (center) is flanked by the oil minister of Kuwait and the emir of Qatar at a 2000 OPEC summit in Caracas, Venezuela. Because of its vast oil reserves, Saudi Arabia has been an influential member of the Organization of Petroleum Exporting Countries since it was founded in 1960.

East, they did send supplies in support of the Arab attackers. In response, the United States sent supplies to its ally Israel.

The conflict threatened to escalate into a major international war involving the world's two most powerful and well-armed nations, the United States and the Soviet Union. A war between the superpowers was avoided, though, after the Americans helped to negotiate a cease-fire. At first, it seemed as if the Yom Kippur episode were over. Afterwards, though, Saudi Arabia and other Arab nations decided to punish the United States and its allies for having helped Israel.

In October 1973, while King Faisal was in power, Saudi Arabia led an OPEC embargo on the sale of oil to the United States and its allies. Oil shipments to the U.S. and the Netherlands were drastically scaled back, and prices for West European buyers were raised some 70 percent.

The embargo caused enormous problems, particularly in the United States, where people depend heavily on oil for so many things, including gasoline for their cars. In the cold of winter,

A meeting of the Gulf Cooperation Council (GCC), which was formed in 1981 by the Arab states of the Arabian Gulf as a way to protect themselves from their larger neighbors, Iran and Iraq. In addition to Saudi Arabia, members of the GCC include Bahrain, Kuwait, Oman, Qatar, and the United Arab Emirates.

Americans were asked to turn down their thermostats in order to conserve heating oil. President Richard Nixon imposed other unpopular gas-saving measures, the most troubling of which were restrictions on the amount of gas service stations could sell.

By the time the embargo was lifted in March 1974, the United States had already devised ways to reduce its dependence on Arab oil. But Saudi Arabia emerged with a new international image. To the West, the desert kingdom was more complex and unpredictable than before. To other Arabs, Saudi Arabia seemed more powerful than it had been previously.

ARAB COALITIONS

Saudi Arabia continued to grow as a strong regional leader. It became increasingly interested in promoting Arab unity so that Arab nations worked together to advance a single goal. To further these efforts, Saudi Arabia formed and/or joined a number of regional organizations.

The Gulf Cooperation Council, founded in 1981, was formed in response to the breakout of the war between Iran and Iraq in September 1980. The charter states that the organization aims, among other things, to maintain security and stability in the region. The council fosters close ties and a certain degree of cultural uniformity, or similarity, between the member states. Members of the Gulf Cooperation Council are Bahrain, Kuwait, Oman, Qatar, Saudi Arabia, and the United Arab Emirates. The Gulf Investment Corporation invests in projects within the Gulf Cooperation Council states.

The 21-member Arab League aims to set common goals, which are somewhat similar to those of the Gulf Cooperation Council. Saudi Arabia acts as both benefactor and leader among the league states. As a nation with great wealth, Saudi Arabia gives financial and other aid to needy Arab countries. Additionally, it attempts to mediate disputes among member nations.

But Saudi Arabia's own relations with its neighbors are complex and sometimes troublesome. At various times, the desert kingdom has broken its ties with its neighbors. In 1979, when Egypt signed a peace agreement with Israel, Saudi Arabia cut off diplomatic relations with Egypt and stopped sending economic aid. Saudi Arabia led a group of other countries in expelling Egypt from the Arab League, and expelled Egyptian workers from the country as well. Egyptian president Anwar el-Sadat took to the airwaves and began broadcasting speeches in which he bitterly denounced the Saudis.

Over the next 10 years, the situation in the Middle East would once again change dramatically. The Soviet Union would invade Afghanistan in 1979, Sadat would be assassinated two years later, Israel would invade Lebanon in 1982, and Iran and Iraq would fight an eight-year-long war. By the end of the 1990s, it seemed more important than ever to keep the region as peaceful and as united as possible. Saudi Arabia wanted to bring Egypt back into the fold of Arab unity. Not wanting to make a direct gesture of friendship, though, the Saudis urged three other nations—Iraq, Jordan, and Sudan—to befriend Egypt again. In 1989, Egypt rejoined the Arab League.

Saudi Arabia has had other problems with its neighbors, including Iran, Iraq, Kuwait, and Jordan. There have been ongoing disputes over borders with Yemen and Oman, other conflicts over the maritime border with Kuwait, and still others with Qatar and the United Arab Emirates.

SAUDI ARABIA AND THE UNITED STATES

The Saudis' most complex foreign relationship is with the United States. That relationship is so convoluted and filled with contradictions and possible problems that even some international affairs experts do not fully understand it.

The United States has been involved with Saudi Arabia since the kingdom was established. American oil companies owned the rights to develop the oil fields they had uncovered in Saudi Arabia. The oil companies knew that at some point, the huge oil reserves could become a major political issue, and could even become the object of a war. The companies asked the U.S. government to help ensure Saudi security.

During World War II, President Franklin D. Roosevelt agreed with the oil companies that Saudi security was important to the United States. In 1943, Roosevelt sent military advisors to train the Saudi army. Roosevelt also dispatched the U.S. Army Corps of Engineers to build a number of military facilities, including an air base at Dhahran, near the coast of the Persian Gulf.

After the war, both the United States and Saudi Arabia believed that the Soviet Union would seize any opportunity it could to gain control of Saudi oil fields. Over the years, as the Soviet Union became more aggressive toward other countries, that belief grew increasingly stronger.

In 1951, Saudi Arabia and the United States formed a special agreement. In exchange for continued access to oilfields, the United States would provide military equipment and training for the Saudi armed forces. The equipment eventually would include high-grade F-15 fighter jets that could repel invading planes. In time, Saudi Arabia's best pilots—even the Saudi ambassador to the United States, Prince Bandar bin Sultan—would be trained by the American military.

The United States followed through on its promise to uphold Saudi security. In 1963, President John F. Kennedy sent American fighter aircraft to Saudi Arabia to help ward off attacks from Egypt. And despite lingering strains over the 1973 OPEC oil embargo and another round of OPEC price increases during the late 1970s,

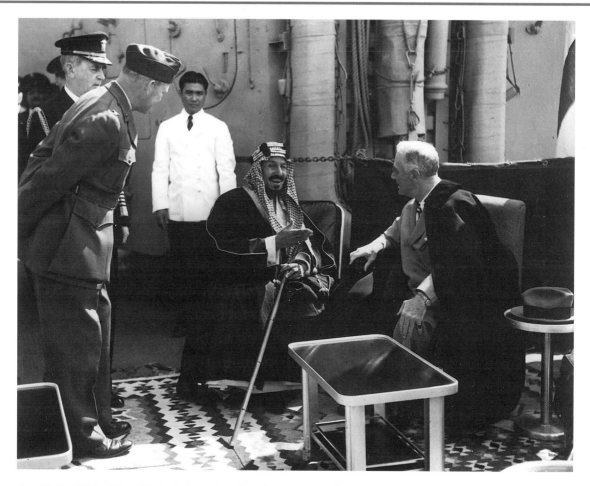

Saudi Arabia's King Abd al-Aziz ibn Saud meets with U.S. President Franklin D. Roosevelt at Great Bitter Lake, Egypt, in February 1945. During the Second World War the U.S. helped train the Saudi army.

President Jimmy Carter continued to uphold the defense pact. In 1980, he loaned a group of highly specialized Airborne Warning and Control System (AWACS) jets to Saudi Arabia. These would give the Saudi military advance notice of attempts to attack the country, so it could fend off any unpleasant surprises.

Behind the friendly gestures between the two countries, however, a deep-seated conflict festered. In 1948, something happened that caused a tremendous strain between the Saudis and the Americans: under a United Nations mandate, a new state of Israel was formed on land once inhabited by the Jews but now inhabited also by Arabs. The Saudis were furious at the decision, and refused to exchange diplomats with Israel or even recognize Israel as a legitimate country. The United States, though, maintained strong support of Israel.

As time progressed, Saudis became more and more convinced that Israel wanted to undermine the U.S.-Saudi relationship. Some politicians in the United States, meanwhile, worried about Saudi Arabia's hostility toward Israel. The U.S. government was already deeply unhappy that Saudi Arabia funded the Palestine Liberation Organization (PLO), a violent anti-Israeli group.

Some in the United States feared that the Saudis would use their U.S.-supplied training and equipment against Israel. The U.S. government decided to cut back—and in some cases, cancel—arms sales to Saudi Arabia. In the eyes of government leaders in Riyadh, it seemed that the United States was abandoning its commitment to defend Saudi Arabia.

Persian Gulf War

In 1990, events in the region once again shook up the balance of Saudi foreign relations. Iraqi leader Saddam Hussein invaded Kuwait. The tiny Persian Gulf nation, tucked inside a bend in the border between Saudi Arabia and Iraq, was completely overrun. The world was appalled. But Saudi Arabia was also frightened. What did Hussein want? What was his ultimate goal? Would Saudi Arabia be next?

The desert kingdom, for all its American-trained pilots and U.S.–supplied equipment, was no match for the belligerent Hussein. Iraq had the fourth-largest army in the world. Additionally, Hussein was known to have developed chemical and biological weapons.

Despite being a recipient of Saudi funding, the Palestine

U.S. and Saudi military personnel survey the damage done to Khobar Towers in 1996. On June 25, a fuel truck exploded outside the facility, which housed U.S. soldiers stationed at King Abd al-Aziz Air Base, near Dhahran; 19 American airmen were killed and more than 370 Americans and Saudis were injured in the attack.

Liberation Organization came out in favor of Hussein. But the United States responded with swift and massive support. In an operation codenamed Desert Shield, America sent more than 400,000 troops to defend Saudi Arabia against a possible attack by Hussein. The news media was filled with images of U.S. infantry soldiers heading off to the Middle East, and of powerful American tanks and equipment being unloaded onto Saudi soil.

Hussein ignored repeated efforts to convince him to withdraw his forces from Kuwait. In February 1991, the United States led a coalition of countries that counterattacked the Iraqi occupation forces and threw them out of Kuwait. Afterwards, Saudi Arabia expressed its gratitude. But it also faced lingering criticism from other Muslim nations unhappy that the government had allowed Western troops into Saudi territory.

RECENT DEVELOPMENTS

Since the Persian Gulf War, Saudi Arabia has outwardly tried to maintain a balance between having good relations with the West while also following the principles and beliefs of Islam.

After the terrorist attacks on September 11, 2001, for example, it emerged that many of the men who hijacked the American planes were Saudi citizens. The terrorists' ringleader, Osama bin Laden, was also a Saudi national. Americans were appalled. Saudi Arabia strongly condemned the horrific acts of September 11. Crown Prince Abdullah responded to the attacks by calling bin Laden a deviant, and he pointed out that the terrorist leader hates Saudi Arabia. Still, many Americans were not convinced of Saudi Arabia's total innocence.

The desert kingdom continues to grapple with issues surrounding the state of Israel. The Saudis want the United States to pressure Israel to withdraw to smaller boundaries, and to allow the formation of a Palestinian state.

In 2002, when Crown Prince Abdullah visited President George W. Bush in Texas, the Israel issue was raised once again. There was talk of yet another oil embargo. Western analysts tried to read between the lines, to determine if the Saudis were actually threatening another embargo; the Saudis said that they were not. And analysts the world over tried even harder to detect clear patterns, and to make sense of the ever-shifting sands of Saudi foreign relations. It was yet another confirmation of the enigmatic personality of this modern kingdom.

CHRONOLOGY

1000 B.C.: People in southern Arabia settle and live in small kingdoms or city-states along the coast or around oases, supporting themselves through oasis farming, herding, or the caravan trade.

5th century A.D.: Mecca becomes the most prominent city in the region.

570: Muhammad, the founder of Islam, is born.

630: Muhammad's army conquers the city of Mecca.

632: Muhammad dies.

632–1500: Islam spreads and flourishes in the Middle East.

15th Century: The Saud dynasty forms in the region of Riyadh.

ca. 1500: Members of the Al Saud clan take control of some date groves near present-day Riyadh, and begin to establish their power there.

1517: Ottomans conquer Egypt, and take control over portions of the Arabian region.

1703: Muslim scholar Muhammad bin Abd al-Wahhab, founder of the Wahhabi sect of Islam, is born.

1744: Wahhab forms an alliance with Muhammad bin Saud of the Al Saud dynasty; the two leaders form an army determined to get rid of the Shia form of Islam, and to instill a more conservative form of Sunni Islam.

1792: Wahhab dies; his teachings continue to take hold among the Al Saud and their followers.

1802: The Wahhabis conquer Mecca.

1812: The Wahhabis are thrown out of Mecca.

1814: Muhammad bin Saud dies; his family continues its alliance with the Wahhabis.

1818: The Wahhabis and the Al Saud, also called the Saudis, further consolidate their power; they establish a capital in Riyadh.

ca. 1865: The political leadership becomes unstable, with much conflict and intrigue between the Al Saud; their rival, the Al-Rashid; and the Turkish Ottomans, who had established a stronghold throughout the surrounding regions.

1891: The Al-Rashid take over Riyadh, forcing the Al Saud into exile in neighboring Kuwait.

CHRONOLOGY

1902: Abd al-Aziz ibn Saud returns from exile and recaptures Riyadh, and over the next 30 years, continues to conquer more territories on the Arabian Peninsula.

1932: The conquered territories are united under the single name, the Kingdom of Saudi Arabia; Abd al-Aziz declares himself king.

1938: Oil is discovered in Saudi Arabia.

1940–45: During World War II, Saudi Arabia supports the Allies (led by the United States and Britain); the U.S. Army builds an air base at Dharhan.

1953: Abd al-Aziz dies and is succeeded by his son, Saud.

1964: King Saud is forced to relinquish power to his brother, Faisal.

1973: Saudi Arabia leads other oil-producing Arab nations in withholding large quantities of oil from Western countries that supported Israel in its war with Egypt; oil prices soar.

1975: King Faisal is murdered, and Khalid becomes king; when Khalid suffers from ill health, his brother Fahd becomes de facto ruler.

1982: Khalid dies, and Fahd becomes king.

1990: Iraq invades Kuwait; in order to protect Saudi Arabia, Fahd welcomes a large contingent of American defense forces into the kingdom.

1991: The United States drives Iraqi invaders out of Kuwait during the brief Gulf War; afterwards, a number of American troops remain on Saudi soil.

mid-1990s: As Fahd's health continues to decline, the duties of king are increasingly assumed by Crown Prince Abdullah.

2001: Islamic militants launch an unprecedented series of terrorist attacks against the United States; many of the terrorists are found to be native Saudis, including the terrorists' leader, Osama bin Laden.

2002: Crown Prince Abdullah is recognized as de facto ruler of Saudi Arabia; in December, Saudi leaders promise the United States their support if war should break out with Iraq.

abayahs—long, flowing gowns covering the entire body from head to toe; they must be worn in public by Saudi women.

Al Rashid—the house of Rashid; the rival family of the Al Saud that competed for control of the Najd region in the 19th century.

Al Saud—the House of Saud; the ruling family of Saudi Arabia.

bedouins—wandering Arab tribesmen.

de facto—operating as a leader, though without official right to do so.

gross domestic product (GDP)—an economic term that measures the flow of domestic goods and services produced by a country within the course of a year.

hajj—a religious pilgrimage to Mecca, which is the duty of all Muslims at least once in their lifetime.

Hejaz—a region in the western part of Saudi Arabia that contains the Muslim holy cities of Medina and Mecca and a chain of mountains along the coast of the Red Sea.

ibn—literally, "son of." Used in a man's name to show that he is son of a particular father, as in, Muhammad ibn Saud. Used interchangeably with "bin."

Ikhwan—a group of desert warriors who followed a very strict form of Islam, and who helped King Abd al-Aziz gain control of the land that would become Saudi Arabia.

majlis—weekly public meetings where male Saudi citizens are allowed to bring their concerns directly before the king or his officials; or, a room where Arab hosts entertain their guests.

Muhammad—the prophet who founded Islam in the early 600s.

Mutawin—religious police who enforce moral and religious laws in Saudi Arabia.

nomads—wanderers; those who have no permanent home but travel from place to place.

Ottoman Empire—a vast empire based in Turkey that began in the early 14th century and lasted until the early 20th century.

Shia—the smaller of the two main branches of Islam. Shiites, who follow the teachings of Shia, are in the minority in Saudi Arabia.

GLOSSARY

souqs—traditional, open-air markets, where buyers and sellers haggle to decide on an item's sale price.

Sunni—the largest of the two main branches of Islam.

ulema—authorities on Islamic law; they have the power to issue rulings based on religious teachings.

wadis—the remains of ancient riverbeds.

Wahhabism—the form of Islam practiced in Saudi Arabia; a strict form of Sunni Islam, established in the mid-1700s by Muhammad ibn Abd al-Wahhab.

Fandy, Mamoun. *Saudi Arabia and the Politics of Dissent.* New York: St. Martin's Press, 2001.

Humphreys, Andrew, et al. *Lonely Planet Middle East.* Oakland, Calif.: Lonely Planet, 2000.

Kechichian, Joseph A. *Succession in Saudi Arabia.* New York: St. Martin's Press, 2001.

Mackey, Sandra. *The Saudis: Inside the Desert Kingdom.* New York: W. W. Norton, 2002.

Metz, Helen Chapin, ed. *Saudi Arabia: A Country Study.* Washington, D.C.: Federal Research Division, Library of Congress, 1993.

Sasson, Jean P. *Princess: A True Story of Life Behind the Veil in Saudi Arabia.* Van Nuys, Calif.: Windsor-Brooke Books, 2001.

Teitelbaum, Joshua. *Holier Than Thou: Saudi Arabia's Islamic Opposition.* Washington, D.C.: Washington Institute for Near East Policy, 2000.

Vassiliev, Alexei. *The History of Saudi Arabia.* New York: New York University Press, 2000.

INTERNET RESOURCES

http://www.lonelyplanet.com/destinations/middle_east/saudi_arabia/

Travel to Saudi Arabia is not easy. You can't just buy a ticket and go. You have to be sponsored by a Saudi national, and even then, you're not guaranteed admission to the country. If you do get sponsored, or even if you don't, but want to get a flavor for the desert kingdom, this site is for you.

http://www.saudinf.com/

The Saudi Ministry of Information maintains this lively site. Here you can find official information on Saudi history, culture, government, and more.

http://www.kingfahdbinabdulaziz.com

Everything you could possibly want to know—and more—about the monarch, King Fahd bin Abd al-Aziz: his life, politics, and accomplishments.

http://www.the-saudi.net/saudi-arabia

This informative site contains information on the history, government, politics, and culture of Saudi Arabia, plus much more. The site contains a link for information on the major cities of Saudi Arabia. Although the info load is not overwhelming (in fact, it's quite spare), the link provides good basic information, and displays photos of the individual cities—including those cities non-Muslims will never see for themselves.

http://www.cia.gov/cia/publications/factbook/geos/sa.html

The Central Intelligence Agency collects up-to-date information and statistics on every country in the world, including Saudi Arabia. Contains chart-style information, plus a country map showing surrounding border areas.

http://www.polisci.com/almanac/world/nation/SA.htm

This on-line political almanac lists facts, statistics, and names. A good resource for when you need to look up a government agency or minister, or find out about trading partners and rates of exchange.

http://www.spa.gov.sa/

A government website in both English and Arabic. Contains current news, plus an interesting link for photographs.

http://www.arabicnews.com/recipes/recipes.html.

A fun site with recipes of traditional foods from the Arab region. For current news, try the site's home page, http://www.arabicnews.com.

INDEX

Numbers in **bold italic** refer to captions.

INDEX

PICTURE CREDITS

CONTRIBUTORS

The **FOREIGN POLICY RESEARCH INSTITUTE (FPRI)** served as editorial consultants for the MODERN MIDDLE EAST NATIONS series. FPRI is one of the nation's oldest "think tanks." The Institute's Middle East Program focuses on Gulf security, monitors the Arab-Israeli peace process, and sponsors an annual conference for teachers on the Middle East, plus periodic briefings on key developments in the region.

Among the FPRI's trustees is a former Secretary of State and a former Secretary of the Navy (and among the FPRI's former trustees and interns, two current Undersecretaries of Defense), not to mention two university presidents emeritus, a foundation president, and several active or retired corporate CEOs.

The scholars of FPRI include a former aide to three U.S. Secretaries of State, a Pulitzer Prize–winning historian, a former president of Swarthmore College and a Bancroft Prize–winning historian, and two former staff members of the National Security Council. And the FPRI counts among its extended network of scholars—especially its Inter-University Study Groups—representatives of diverse disciplines, including political science, history, economics, law, management, religion, sociology, and psychology.

DR. HARVEY SICHERMAN is president and director of the Foreign Policy Research Institute in Philadelphia, Pennsylvania. He has extensive experience in writing, research, and analysis of U.S. foreign and national security policy, both in government and out. He served as Special Assistant to Secretary of State Alexander M. Haig Jr. and as a member of the Policy Planning Staff of Secretary of State James A. Baker III. Dr. Sicherman was also a consultant to Secretary of the Navy John F. Lehman Jr. (1982–1987) and Secretary of State George Shultz (1988).

A graduate of the University of Scranton (B.S., History, 1966), Dr. Sicherman earned his Ph.D. at the University of Pennsylvania (Political Science, 1971), where he received a Salvatori Fellowship. He is author or editor of numerous books and articles, including *America the Vulnerable: Our Military Problems and How to Fix Them* (FPRI, 2002) and *Palestinian Autonomy, Self-Government and Peace* (Westview Press, 1993). He edits *Peacefacts*, an FPRI bulletin that monitors the Arab-Israeli peace process.

SUSAN KATZ KEATING is an educator and freelance writer. A former newspaper reporter and editor, she specializes in military and national security issues. Her work has appeared in *Readers Digest*, *George*, *American Legion*, the *New York Times*, and other publications. She is the author of *Prisoners of Hope: Exploiting the POW/MIA Myth in America* (Random House, 1994), as well as several books for young readers. The mother of three children, she lives with her family and pets in Virginia, where she is a 4-H Club leader and helps to run a 4-H horse club.